DRIVE RIGHT IN

Vehicle Access for the Real Estate Professional

By Joseph Schaefer

Drive Right In

ISBN 978-0-9910703-5-0

Library of Congress Control Number: 2013952471

Published by:
Wilsonville Media, Wilsonville, Oregon
www.WilsonvilleMedia.com

Contact the author at www.DriveRightInBook.com

Book design by www.WilsonvilleMedia.com
Illustrations by www.brokenboxdesigns.com

CONTENTS

ABOUT THE AUTHOR

JOSEPH SCHAEFER

Joseph Schaefer has worked in various aspects of real estate for over 20 years, including projects in construction, code enforcement, eminent domain, asset management, and entitlements. His particular interest is functional site planning, especially regarding the relationship between buildings and properties and their unique neighborhood settings. He holds a BA from St. Lawrence University and a Masters in Urban and Regional Planning from Portland State University. He serves as Chairman of the Planning Commission in Aurora, Oregon. This is his first book.

ACKNOWLEDGEMENTS

Three people provided invaluable assistance in transforming the rough manuscript into the finished book. As Editor, Don Donovan brought the practical perspective of an experienced regulator, and was especially helpful with the chapters on access management and driveway design. As Illustrator, Wendy Sefcik of Broken Box Designs was simply superb in her ability to succinctly present technical concepts. Bud Fawcett is a master of electronic publishing, and really is the person who brought the book from me to you.

Always design a thing by considering it in its next larger context — a chair in a room, a room in a house, a house in an environment, an environment in a city plan.

Eliel Saarinen

INTRODUCTION

Why this book? One day a thorny shopping center access problem confronted me. It occurred that others had surely faced this situation before, so there must be a good resource out there with instructive advice. An extensive search revealed comprehensive civil engineering textbooks, a tall stack of government studies, policies and regulations, and a couple parking lot tomes, all of which provided useful information without much practical guidance. The curriculum for my Masters Degree in urban planning offered nothing. Books about real estate development devote a couple paragraphs to the subject at most, while appraisals of commercial real estate often get by with a sentence or two.

What I didn't find was anything substantial that speaks to vehicle access from perspectives other than traffic engineers and government regulators. Nor did I find a review of the access issues applicable to different types of real estate. So, I asked around, and none of my colleagues had seen anything like this either. When questioned how they learned about access, the usual responses were on the job training, or a simple shrug of the shoulders, sometimes followed by a wry smile.

This book is intended as a practical guide for students and the full variety of real estate professionals, including government regulators and traffic engineers. While access is most crucial for retail property, all types of properties benefit from good access, and can be harmed, sometimes severely, by poor access.

Access problems and solutions are ultimately about how well the alignment of streets and driveways functions around developed real estate. There is much geometry, especially angles, arcs, and radii, and distances of many types, such as sight distance, stopping distance, queue length, throat distance, and others. If an access is being built or rearranged, engineering drawings will be required, whether custom drawings or something off the transportation agency's shelf. The reader is introduced to the technical jargon in context, without getting bogged down in the engineering specifications. The idea is to explain the essential concepts and terms so that you can converse smartly with the engineers doing the detailed design, and the regulators that must approve it.

Vehicle access is extensively regulated by government transportation agencies at all levels. The regulatory principles and terminology are presented, with emphasis on regulatory changes; for example, when a street is widened. Changes in streets and their regulations create winners and losers, and the reader will learn about which types of property are likely to fall into each category, which is perhaps the most significant topic within this book. Access can also be governed by private arrangement; for example, in larger shopping centers, where savvy retailers get it in writing to protect themselves against deleterious changes made by both regulators and landlords.

Part 1 explains basic principles that surround access issues. It begins with contemporary street classifications and intersections. The various professions and perspectives involved in access are reviewed. A chapter on access management describes access restrictions (and prohibitions) on higher (read wider) classifications of streets, and what happens when new access management policies are applied to an existing commercial street. Chapters on due diligence and access rights explain the nitty gritty of researching the regulations and rights that govern a particular property. The chapter on traffic studies covers this key precursor to both private development and government projects such as creation of a new street. A summary of driveway design concludes Part 1.

Part 2 describes access issues particular to different land uses. Regardless of land use, a good access must be simple and intuitive. A lengthy glossary is provided to demystify the technical terms.

We've all been cruising in and out of driveways since we were teenagers, without thinking much about it. Once I described the complexity of a business park access problem and its importance for that property to a friend.

Her response was: Who knew? Now you will.

Success is neither magical nor mysterious. Success is the natural consequence of consistently applying the basic fundamentals.

Jim Rohn

PART 1 – PRINCIPLES

There are key fundamental concepts influencing access, and as a first principle, the concepts are driven by the right-of-way classification. At one end of the spectrum, local streets, whether residential, commercial or industrial, provide vehicle access for individual properties. At the opposite end, freeways do not provide access to any individual properties, rather only to other public rights-of-way. Next we briefly examine intersection types, and their respective strengths and weaknesses. Many types of real estate professionals participate in vehicle access, and they each bring predictable opinions to the table. Understanding who these people are and how they approach access is crucial to breaking down the particular problems, and negotiating positive outcomes.

Then transportation agency policies are covered in the chapter on access management, where access restrictions (and prohibitions) are explained. The application of new access management regulations to existing commercial streets is also considered.

Chapters on due diligence and access rights demonstrate how to research the regulations and legal rights to a particular property. Because access can be controlled both by public regulations and private agreements, there is no substitute for doing the extensive homework required to learn the specific rights and restrictions that pertain to property.

Traffic studies inform and constrain private development and government projects alike. They have a huge impact on where and how access is provided, and knowing their quirks provides an insider's view of how the studies influence access location and design. After the preliminary negotiations about traffic flow and driveway location are complete, then the design is drawn. Driveway design elements are presented and illustrated.

1

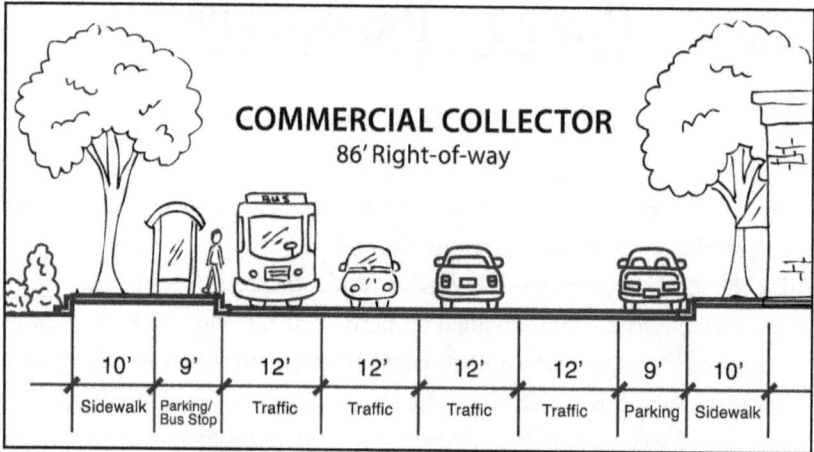

COMMERCIAL COLLECTOR
86' Right-of-way

10'	9'	12'	12'	12'	12'	9'	10'
Sidewalk	Parking/Bus Stop	Traffic	Traffic	Traffic	Traffic	Parking	Sidewalk

CHAPTER ONE

STREET TYPES AND CLASSIFICATIONS

All streets are classified by their intended function, as administered by the responsible transportation agency. Access is one of three key elements of street classifications, with design speed and traffic volume being the other two.

Each classification has distinct access standards, and the requirements for any given driveway are driven by the classification of the street where the driveway is located. "Higher" classifications including freeways, highways, and arterials, move more traffic by limiting access. The "lower" classifications of collectors and local streets provide more access even if that slows traffic. Be sure to learn the current and any potential future classification for any street of interest.

FREEWAYS

Starting at the top, freeways only allow vehicle access at public interchanges where acceleration and deceleration ramps are provided. Freeways are grade separated, meaning that all crossing streets (and railroads) are either an overpass above, or an underpass below. The federal interstate system is all freeway, and some segments of U.S. and state highways are freeways as well. Expressway is another word for highways with limited access, and while the term includes some freeways, other "expressways" are not freeways.

Access to a freeway interchange is almost always from a public street or another freeway. The only exceptions are limited to the largest and usually institutional uses, such as an airport or a large sports stadium. Even then, the access street from the interchange into the facility is classified as a public street, if only for formality's sake.

Freeways are largely managed by state departments of transportation. The federal government holds the purse strings. The Federal Highway Administration regulates the states, but prefers to remain in the background, and is typically limited to overseeing state and regional transportation agency actions. Approval for an interchange is obtained from the state department of transportation.

STATE AND U.S. HIGHWAYS

The second highest classification is State and U.S. Highways. Prior to creation of the interstates, U.S. Highways were the highest classification, and most state highways were also first built prior to the interstate freeways. Over the decades they evolved in all sorts of ways, to the point where some parts operate more like freeways, and others more like main streets. The states have substantial discretion about how to manage them, even the U.S. Highways.

Where State and U.S. Highways pass through towns and cities, their management can get muddled, and multiple agencies will likely be involved. They will have a second classification in these segments, such as urban arterial. That is, the state and federal governments may classify a U.S. Highway as just that, and a city may classify it as an arterial street. Access permits for both State and U.S. highways are obtained through the state transportation agency that has specialized staff just for that purpose, and additional (even if it seems duplicative) permits may be required from the city or county as well.

ARTERIALS

Arterial streets are designed for five lanes or wider. Their function is to move traffic over larger distances within urban areas, and bring the traffic to and from regional facilities, such as freeways. Access is often limited or prohibited. A good example of arterial streets where (almost) no private access is allowed is MacArthur Boulevard in Santa Ana, California which is just southeast of the John Wayne airport.

Many cities distinguish between major and minor arterials as well. Arterials may be controlled by the state, county, or city, so you will need to ask to be sure, and don't be surprised if the responsibilities overlap. One agency may own the right-of-way, while another has administrative control.

When arterial streets cross through single-family residential neighborhoods, the lots usually take access from a local street parallel to the arterial. The exception is in older neighborhoods where the street was not originally planned as an arterial.

COLLECTORS

The next step down from arterials is collectors, whose function is to collect traffic from local streets and carry it to nearby local attractions, such as a suburban downtown, and to the arterial system. Collectors range from two to four lanes wide. There are usually traffic signals where collectors meet arterials.

Collectors are sometimes classified according to the land use they serve, such as an industrial collector, or a residential collector. These designations drive the design. For example, an industrial collector will emphasize space for truck turns more than pedestrian facilities, while a residential collector does the opposite.

For access, collectors lie in the middle between the higher classifications where property access is discouraged or prohibited and the lower classification of local streets where all properties get access. Access is generally provided on a collector street, but when a property has frontage on both a local street and a collector, the transportation agency may insist that access be taken from the local street.

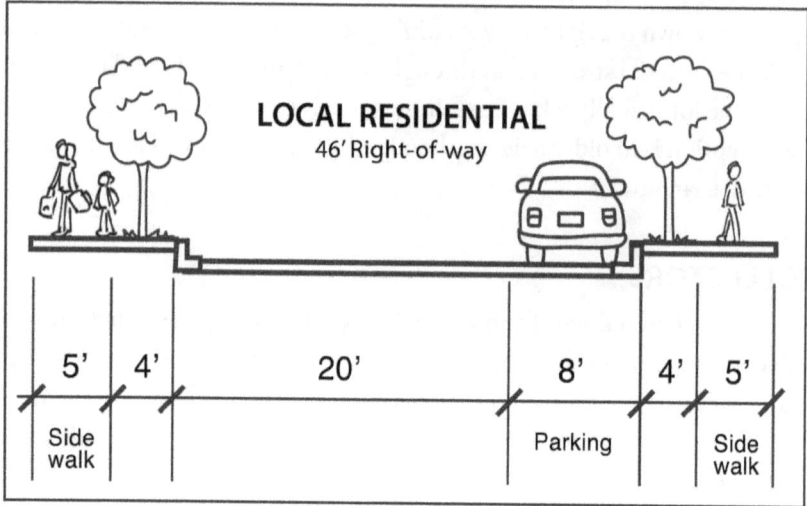

LOCAL STREETS

Local streets are intended to provide vehicle access to all abutting properties. They are also sometimes classified according to the land use they serve, which again influences the design. There are very few local streets serving office and retail property, because these land uses generate more traffic than is desired on local streets. There are, however, many residential and industrial neighborhoods served by local streets.

CHANGES IN CLASSIFICATION

Often public right-of-way begins as a local street, and as an area develops more densely, some streets are selected for upgrading to collectors or arterials. When funding is found, the upgraded streets are then widened. In other words, the classification of a street is not always apparent on the ground because it is often aspirational. Transportation planning is a very long term enterprise, and funds for widening streets are limited. If the street has a higher classification than it is currently built to, the transportation agency intends to widen it. Maybe not tomorrow or next year, but some day.

The list of planned street projects vastly exceeds available funding. If the street serving your property is on the project list, find the knowledgeable public officials, and call them once a year to check on whether the project is moving up on the list. It's the best way to avoid a problematic surprise.

Rarely is the classification of a street lowered, and typically, it requires a major change that substantially reduces traffic. For example, if a new freeway is built which blocks the path of a collector street, it may be downgraded to a local street.

TABLE OF RADIUS CURB DIMENSIONS

	Arterial Street	Collector Street	Local Street	Driveway
Arterial Street	30'	25'	25'	25'
Collector Street	25'	25'	25'	25'
Local Street	25'	25'	18'	18'
Driveway	25'	25'	18'	18'

CHAPTER TWO

INTERSECTIONS

Vehicles traveling to your property first pass through intersections, and for many larger properties, an intersection serves as the entrance. The central theme is that good access should be simple and intuitive for the ease and comfort of your visitors. Intersections that operate smoothly minimize demands on drivers' attention by eliminating conflicting movements, so they can focus on signage, properties, and access.

Stop-controlled intersections obviously have the lowest traffic capacity. Roundabouts have more capacity than stop-controlled intersections, but less than signalized intersections, and of course, signalized intersections can accommodate large to huge amounts of traffic. There are general principles that apply to all three.

The influence area (or functional area) of an intersection is the distance upstream (leading to the intersection) and downstream (leading away from the intersection) on each leg of the intersection that is "influenced" by intersection operations. On the upstream leg, the influence area begins where vehicles first see and react to a decision point, such as a red light or widening for a left turn storage lane. On the downstream leg, the area includes the distance required for merging of the turning vehicles and acceleration.

Traffic engineers strive to keep driveways away from intersection influence areas to prevent conflicts from vehicles entering and exiting the street. It's important to know what the local transportation agency thinks the length of the influence area is along the property frontage. Recognize that the area may grow over time as traffic increases. For many developed properties, driveways are already located within an influence area. It gets awkward when the transportation agency considers your customers and vendors as conflicts, and driveways within an influence area are most at risk of closure.

STOP-CONTROLLED INTERSECTIONS

From the driver's perspective, there are two types of stop-controlled intersections: those where the cross traffic also stops, and those where it does not. Where the cross traffic also stops, drivers can relax since there will not be any vehicles traveling through the intersection at speed. This allows more opportunity to view surrounding properties. The key thing to consider is the view of a property – and its entrance – from vehicles both approaching the stop sign and accelerating through the intersection. In other words, consider how the property appears to passersby moving slowly to and through the intersection.

Of course, when the cross traffic does not stop, the drivers' attention is occupied with that traffic, and less attention can be given to surrounding properties. The degree of attention affects reaction times, and thus driveway placement should account for it. Practically speaking, if drivers have just crossed through a harrowing intersection, they need a little more time and distance before they can comfortably recognize and enter a driveway. For downstream driveways, if the traffic stopped at the intersection, the vehicles will be accelerating, and there will be gaps between them. In this situation, it's fine to have a right-in driveway close to the corner because at that point the vehicles will still be moving slowly.

When vehicles pass through an intersection where only the cross traffic stops, they may slow down, or may proceed through the intersection at speed. In this situation, there is less time to see the driveway early enough to slow down while passing through the intersection and pull into the driveway, so it's better for the driveway to be further away from the corner. These suggestions all depend on the speed limit and the speed of traffic, as faster speeds require more time and distance for drivers to react to seeing the driveway and decelerate in order to enter it.

ROUNDABOUTS

Roundabouts are gaining acceptance in the United States, largely because they fill the gap where there is too much traffic for stop signs, but not enough for a signal. Roundabouts only cost a quarter as much as signals to build, and there is no expensive equipment to maintain. They also reduce the number and severity of crashes, due to lower speeds in the intersection and the oblique angles at which crashes occur. Expect to see more of them in the coming years.

As with all types of intersections, driveways that are too close to roundabouts are difficult to get in and out of. The whole point of a roundabout is that traffic does not stop, and thus when the intersection is busy, there are no gaps between vehicles which can be used to exit from a property, or to turn left into it. This is a serious problem on the downstream side of the roundabout, in part because the drivers relax and accelerate once they are finally clear of the roundabout, and they were not been able to see any driveways while going through it.

Consider the circling and the decisions each driver must make while navigating. A driver in a roundabout must constantly watch for vehicles merging, which draws attention from nearby driveways or signs. This differs from stop signs and signalized intersections, where vehicles are channelized into lanes, merging is less frequent, and there are moments to pause and look around.

SIGNALIZED INTERSECTIONS

Signalized intersections do a fantastic job of choreographing vehicles traveling in different directions through the same space to maximize traffic flow (and safety). Larger properties in suburban areas ideally have direct access from a signalized intersection. Retail properties of ten acres or larger definitely should have a signalized entrance. While signals are expensive, lost customers who pass by the property because they cannot comfortably see the signage and enter the driveway are even more expensive. A driveway entrance that is one leg of a signalized intersection minimizes the number of decision points confronting a driver, and the turn into the property is simple and intuitive.

Traffic signal cycles are managed by an electronic controller, which is located in an unmarked metal cabinet placed on the sidewalk near the corner. The controller receives information from signal loops, which are metal detectors embedded in the pavement on the upstream legs of an intersection. Signal loops sense how many vehicles are in a specific lane, and software in the controller adapts the signal timing to accommodate the traffic. For example, at the small signalized intersection near my home, if one vehicle is in the left turn lane, the left turn green arrow does not come on until the end of the cycle, but if more than one vehicle is in the left turn lane, the left turn green arrow comes on sooner.

Controllers are programmable, and thus, can be adjusted. Naturally they attempt to balance the traffic coming from all directions, but the traffic does not always flow as anticipated. If an intersection at or near your property has unusually long wait times for one movement, contact the local transportation agency about adjusting the controller.

Lane striping and traffic signs are also adjustable, though not as easily. Again, the thing to watch for is a movement with unusual delays. Perhaps a lane designated for left turns and through traffic should be designated for left turns only; perhaps a second left turn lane is necessary. Upstream vehicles intend to make one of three movements: left turn (including u-turns), continue straight, or right turn. The more efficiently the vehicles can get into the appropriate lane, the better. Of course, the contrary is true, that if the different lanes for going left, straight or right are not clearly indicated, vehicles are merging or weaving as they approach the intersection, and traffic will not flow smoothly. Driveways near intersections cause this type of merging and weaving, which is why they are discouraged.

Signal progression is where a series of signals are timed to allow vehicles to travel through several intersections without stopping. This is especially important at rush hour. However, many merchants frown on signal progression, because it encourages vehicles to cruise past their property at full speed. Fewer people have the time to view signage and buildings, and fewer are comfortable slowing down to enter a driveway with lots of traffic coming behind them. The counterargument is that without signal progression, congestion will cause vehicles to seek alternate routes, and after all, the flow of rush hour traffic is a much higher priority for the transportation agency.

Ideally all the vehicles waiting at a red light move through the intersection during the next green light as a group, and that group is called a platoon. If some vehicles don't make it, this is called spillback.

FREEWAY INTERCHANGES

Convenient freeway access is a magnet for large-scale real estate development which seeks to take advantage of the convenience. This is the most scrutinized and regulated type of access there is and involves multiple transportation agencies.

In prior decades, the line between regional traffic and local traffic was drawn where the entrance and exit ramps met the cross street. Over time, as traffic congestion increased around interchanges, transportation engineers realized there were two basic types of trips around interchanges: local trips and regional trips. The function of a freeway is for long distance trips at high speed, whereas local trips, of course, are shorter trips at lower speed. Congestion around interchanges occurs in part because the slower local trips interfere with the higher speed longer trips. The solution to that congestion is to increase the volume and speed of traffic around interchanges, but that cannot occur where there are private driveways and street intersections close to the interchange.

To make traffic around interchanges flow smoothly, complete control of access to the interstate and its ramps is not sufficient. Access control on cross streets near an interchange is also vital. Thus, in recent years, transportation agencies expanded the geographic area under consideration when reviewing access near interchanges. Stringent access management on the cross street serving an interchange has become an essential part of interchange design.

For each proposed modification to an interchange, the Federal Highway Administration (FHWA) and State Department of Transportation (DOT) negotiate the geographic area to analyze, which is then considered the influence area. The influence area typically extends more than a half-mile in each direction along the cross street leading to the interchange ramps, and a quarter-mile in each direction perpendicular from the cross street. In other words, it is a rectangle more than a mile wide perpendicular to the interstate and a half-mile wide parallel to it. The properties within the influence area are at risk of access alterations.

The closer a property is to an interchange, the greater the risk of access alterations. If a property has driveway access onto the cross street, it is at risk of closure, because transportation agencies prefer that no properties within the influence area take access from the cross street. The strong preference is for driveway access to be onto local streets that lead to signalized intersections with the cross street, and for those intersections to be placed as far as possible from the ramps. In other words, the fewer driveways and street intersections on the cross street, the better. You can see how this preference favors larger properties near interchanges, because these properties can consolidate access at signalized intersections.

Frontage streets along freeways have fallen out of fashion, because their intersections with the cross street are near the interstate ramps and cause too much congestion. Properties which utilize a frontage street that intersects with the cross street near the interchange ramps are at risk, even in the absence of a large interchange project. The intersection of the frontage street and the cross street may be closed, or limited to right turns only, forcing long detours.

During modification of an interchange, major access changes are certain to occur because the government will not invest huge sums in a modified interchange if the surrounding street network will be too congested to take advantage of that investment. The agencies determine the increased volume of traffic to design for, and then redesign both the interchange and the surrounding street network to handle that volume.

Redesign of the street network within the influence area to handle more traffic inevitably means access closures and restrictions. The design goal is to separate interchange traffic from traffic that is going to or from a local destination; i.e., individual properties, and within the influence area the smooth flow of interchange traffic is the top priority. Therefore, private driveways and public street intersections serving local property are seen as impediments.

Of course, many vehicles use cross streets for local trips, but these are the bane of interchange designers. Not many jurisdictions can afford to build an overpass separate from the interchange just to handle local trips, so the interchanges are pressed into double duty, and congestion ensues. Because the interchange gets priority, the solution is to reduce access to the cross street, and vehicles headed to locations near the interchange are left to navigate a circuitous route.

For example, look at the interchange of Jamboree Rd. with the San Diego Freeway (I-405) about a half mile east of the Orange County Airport. Within a mile of the interchange there are just a couple access driveways to Jamboree Rd. Both are restricted to right turns. Then look at the office buildings on the frontage street, McCabe Way, just northeast of the interchange. The intersection of McCabe Way and Jamboree Rd. is now closed, and vehicles traveling to and from the office buildings must use a circuitous route. Note these are office buildings, a destination use. Retail could not survive in the same location. Bear in mind this is one of the busiest interstates in the country, and can be considered an outlier. However, it represents the state of the art and is a good illustration of where private access driveways are almost nonexistent near the interchange, and public street intersections are also few and far between.

All the world's a stage and all the men and women merely players.

William Shakespeare

CHAPTER THREE
THE PLAYERS

There are always at least two parties involved in vehicle access to a public street: the property owner and the transportation agency official. The maximum number can grow to fill a conference room, especially with public involvement in a controversial case. This chapter describes the players and their roles, scripts, and perspectives.

GOVERNMENT OFFICIALS

The size of the transportation agency responsible for the right-of-way drives the degree of specialization within the agency staff. For rights-of-way controlled by local governments, even the smallest jurisdictions will likely have a civil engineer, if only on a consulting basis. The civil engineer handles design details such as curb design, the width of the access, and pedestrian crossings. They also inspect the work as it progresses. This person is likely to present a standard design and expect the access to conform in most, if not all, particulars. In a small jurisdiction the same civil engineer will also handle access management standards and storm drainage.

A medium-size suburb will likely have a technician to handle routine access permits. When there is concern about the location of an access, a transportation planner is likely to be involved. The transportation planner helps administer the access spacing standards and should be familiar with any long range plans for changes to the right-of-way. While their role is to enforce the access spacing standards vigorously, the degree of flexibility varies widely among jurisdictions.

Medium-size suburbs may also have a traffic engineer responsible for review of traffic studies provided by any consulting traffic engineers (working for either the government or property parties). The traffic engineer decides (or makes recommendations to the city engineer) about traffic flow such as selection of design vehicles (which determines lane widths and the shape of access points), speed limits, and placement of traffic signals.

These people work within the city's engineering department under the supervision of the city engineer (or in smaller cities, under the public works director). The city engineer typically reports to a city manager regarding complaints and other sensitive matters, such as cost sharing for a traffic signal, and condemnation cases.

Above the city manager are the elected officials. The city manager and elected officials may or may not understand the details of a particular access problem, and may simply rely on the engineering staff to inform them. They are unlikely to be seen at the job site, whereas, engineering staff will be seen there.

The larger the local government, the less likely that the city manager and elected officials will appear at the conference table. One important role of city managers is to insulate elected officials from controversy, and keeping them away from meetings with complex subject matter is one way to accomplish that. Of course their not being there is likely to delay any decision. The key question is whether the people with real authority will join the meeting, so find out who actually makes these decisions. Is the management style of the current elected officials hands on, or do they prefer to delegate?

The public works department will have someone review the design and monitor the construction schedule. This department is responsible for the access after it is built, and wants to ensure that the design is practical for maintenance.

If the right-of-way is a state facility, both state and local officials will be involved. In addition to the local officials described above, the state transportation department will have several staff members. Most state transportation departments are divided into districts, with offices spread throughout the state. The local offices will likely also have different people to review the traffic engineering details, the civil engineering details, the access management standards, and storm drainage.

If the right-of-way is a federal highway or interstate highway, the Federal Highway Administration (FHWA) delegates the operational management to the State Department of Transportation (DOT). FHWA officials tend to remain in the background, though if significant changes are proposed to an interstate highway, the State DOT must submit a comprehensive application to them. You are unlikely to meet federal officials unless you are directly involved with changes to the interstate.

The fire department plan review staff scrutinizes projects to ensure that emergency vehicles can swiftly reach all buildings. They expect strict compliance with the Uniform Fire Code, and have an appeals process when that is not possible. If a project is unable to provide their large trucks with excellent access, expect to invest in extra alarms, building exits, hydrants, and sprinklers.

The script for most staff level public officials is that any proposal must meet adopted access standards for safety and the smooth flow of traffic. They are paid to administer and enforce laws, regulations, and the access standards adopted pursuant thereto, and typically lack authority to flexibly accommodate any special needs of the private sector. Middle and higher level public officials will have the authority to be flexible in limited circumstances, especially when a proposal falls within a grey area. From their perspective, a proposal that clearly conflicts with straightforward regulations is unlikely to be persuasive.

The top level officials, meaning agency heads, city managers, and elected or appointed bodies such as a city council or state agency board, are in the habit of following the recommendations of staff. If you need them to bend the rules, understand they will be initially reluctant, and be prepared to demonstrate that their goals for safety and traffic flow can be reached with your alternative proposal.

THE PROPERTY OWNER

The property owner strives for the best possible access at the least possible cost. Sometimes this person is an experienced real estate executive, at other times it will be a novice. Realize that the owner, or whoever represents the owner, probably answers to several other parties, such as lenders, tenants and investors.

The property owner will almost invariably advocate for access that allows left turns. For Class A, and the more valuable Class B properties, most owners are willing to invest in additional lanes and traffic signals to improve access.

For less valuable properties, and projects run by novices, the owner may prefer to do without what they see as unnecessary amenities, or insist that the transportation agency foot the bill. These people are earnest and may fight hard, but frankly their locations often are not viable independently on streets with higher traffic volumes. Their best solution is often to aggregate their property with others, but their lack of real estate expertise can make this unlikely. Many of these properties need to be scraped for redevelopment in a new form that can function well on wider streets.

PROPERTY MANAGERS

Many property owners hire property management companies to run their properties and deal with regulatory issues like access. The property manager is typically paid a percentage of the property revenue, and will not be paid extra for their time and effort to deal with an access problem. They will often tell the owner that consultants should be hired, and will desire a quick and simple solution.

At the same time, experienced managers will be very sensitive to the potential adverse impacts of access changes. If not at first, they will be after catching an earful from concerned tenants. Loss or reduction of access—even temporarily—translates into vacancies, rent concessions, and reduced property management fees. Property managers recognize the importance of quality access, and a quick and simple solution that hurts the access will not be seen by them as a viable solution at all.

Another dynamic is that for many commercial properties, common area maintenance expenses (CAMs) are billed to tenants. That is, the costs of many access changes are paid by the tenants, not the property owner. The property manager needs to juggle both the total cost and the allocation of the costs between owners and tenants. For example, the owner might be responsible for the construction cost of a new access (as a capital improvement), but the tenants may be responsible for the additional future cost of maintaining it (paving, striping, drainage, landscaping, etc.).

TENANTS

Large retail chains have sophisticated real estate managers and consulting engineers to handle the design and development of new stores. For changes to an existing access, the store manager will contact them and defer to them, but they are very busy people responsible for many stores over wide geographic areas. It might be difficult to get their attention, but once you have it, they are usually quite swift on the uptake.

Smaller tenants may lack real estate experience, and be slower to understand the significance of access issues, or they will understand it and respond emotionally. They fear lost business during construction, and that they may not have sufficiently deep pockets to survive the project. They fear that after construction, they will lose business because of changes in the access. Often the fears are totally justified, and business failures are common during and after street improvement projects.

THE TITLE COMPANY

Access rights are supposed to be spelled out in public records, and the title company's role is to compile that record. (In some parts of the country lawyers do much of the title research.) The title report will list as special exceptions the recorded documents that affect access rights, such as easements, plats, leases, and conveyance (and vacation) of right-of-way. The title officer will circulate the report and supporting documents, which are then analyzed by affected parties (most often surveyors and real estate lawyers) to determine the specific access rights that are in place. The title company compiles the record of applicable documents; however, it is not their job to explain the meaning of those documents to you, and they will usually be careful not to do so.

PRIVATE REAL ESTATE LAWYER

The role of the real estate lawyer retained by the property owner is to analyze the title documents and surveys to ascertain the access rights, and then to insist that the transportation agency respect those property rights, or pay to acquire them. For larger properties, this lawyer may serve as the property owner's representative in negotiations with the transportation agency, at public hearings, and in negotiations with other parties, such as a neighbor with reciprocal easement rights. The lawyer should be experienced with the particular state and local laws regarding access. As a practical matter, this means they should specialize in the development or redevelopment of commercial real estate. Many commercial real estate lawyers concentrate on transactions for existing commercial properties and lack significant experience with development or redevelopment, and thus with access problems. In larger jurisdictions, some attorneys even specialize in access.

When selecting an attorney, understand their attitude toward the transportation agency, and make certain it is consistent with your own. Some attorneys maintain cozy relationships with transportation agencies, and will not jeopardize those long term relationships to forcefully advocate for a single client, especially if litigation becomes necessary. Others specialize in litigation to protect the rights of property owners, but may lack the technical knowledge, or be too intimidating to negotiate a functional compromise with the transportation agency staff. In some instances you may need both types; the well-connected type to attempt a compromise, and later, a litigator if the attempt is unsuccessful.

GOVERNMENT REAL ESTATE LAWYER

On the government side, the transportation agency will have an attorney when it must acquire property, typically to widen a street, expand an intersection, or close an access. Often this attorney will remain in the background, at least in the early stages, but expect that they will prepare the documents that agency staff or the right-of-way agent asks you to sign.

If negotiations fail or get complicated, this lawyer will move to the foreground. Their job is to complete the transaction for the lowest possible price to the government. When disputes arise over what access rights are held by a property, their job is to insist that the rights asserted by the property owner either do not exist, or are not worth very much money. Their client is the transportation agency which insists that access be limited or closed in order to improve the function of the right-of-way; the success or failure of businesses is not their concern.

Difficult cases occasionally are litigated, where it is likely a different government lawyer will handle the court case.

THE RIGHT-OF-WAY AGENT

When a transportation agency needs to acquire right-of-way, the right-of-way agent is responsible for buying the various (and often numerous) pieces from the property owners. This person coordinates the engineering drawings, the appraisal, and the conveyance documents, and most importantly, negotiates with the property owners.

Transportation agencies do varying amounts of this work in-house, so this right-of-way person may be a regular agency employee. There are also specialized companies and consultants that do this work on a contract basis for government agencies. The role is the same. These people are responsible for pitching property owners on the benefits of the project, and especially on the price they are offering for the real estate (including access rights) being acquired. If this person cannot close the deal, the lawyer for the government agency will step in and condemnation follows.

THE SURVEYOR

The surveyor's role is to map the existing or proposed access and access restrictions. For new development, the surveyor will prepare the base map of the property boundary, including topography. If the land is being divided, the surveyor will prepare the plat. When streets or access easements are created or altered in the course of a land division, the details will be shown on the plat. The plat will also show areas where access has been formally restricted (read prohibited). Prior to construction, the surveyor will mark the exact location of the access driveway elements, such as the curbs.

For existing development, lenders often require an ALTA Survey, which is the most comprehensive type of survey. It will show all the existing development in great detail, as well as easements of record in the title report, and easements and restrictions from prior plats, including those affecting access. In sum, an ALTA Survey maps all the recorded access rights affecting a property. Watch for easements in the access area; these can obstruct access when utility work is required.

All of these surveys use the title report as a base reference. Always check the date of the title report listed on the survey. If it is more than a month or two before the date of the survey itself, it may not include the most recent recorded documents.

Note that a boundary survey (or an architect's site plan) will not show access rights and restrictions.

THE CONSULTING TRAFFIC ENGINEER

For a new development, the consulting traffic engineer works for the developer and writes a report on traffic flow around the property before and after the project. The traffic engineer recommends a conceptual design with basic information like the access locations, the number of lanes, and the design vehicle, and ensures that street traffic does not obstruct the access, and vice versa. Most consulting traffic engineers rely on government agencies for the bulk of their business, and should not be expected to advocate vigorously in opposition to those agencies.

For a public works project initiated by a transportation agency, such as a street widening, the traffic engineer works for the transportation agency, often as an outside consultant. The traffic report typically analyzes a street segment and its access points, both private access driveways and public intersections. The report will recommend the number of lanes, the specific locations and types of intersections, and the specific locations of driveways, etc.

Most traffic engineers employed in house by transportation agencies serve an advisory role, with larger projects being contracted out to private firms.

THE CONSULTING CIVIL ENGINEER

The consulting civil engineer may work for a private developer in the case of new development, or the transportation agency. This person takes the conceptual design provided by the traffic engineer, and fleshes it out over several drafts into detailed construction drawings. The drafts are identified by the percentage of completion. Thirty percent (30%) drawings have sufficient detail for negotiating the important attributes of an access, such as location, width, and signalization, as well as for right-of-way acquisition and preliminary cost estimates. If you wait until later drafts to get involved, it may be too late to influence the location and basic design of access points. Those later drafts will fill in more engineering details, but are unlikely to alter the major features of an access.

THE CONTRACTOR

The contractor brings the work of all the other participants to fruition in the field. Their primary concerns are the accuracy and detailing of the design drawings, and the difficulty of construction. They are on the alert for impractical designs, and when they speak about this, it is important to listen. However, they provide the most value in this regard when they are included in early design discussions. Topographical details are vitally important to the contractor because minor changes in grade have substantial cost implications, and if anything goes wrong, such as a sag grade or stormwater puddles, everyone calls (and blames) them first. The greater the slope, the more important it is to get the contractor involved early.

ACCESS MANAGEMENT TECHNIQUES

Install median barrier with no direct left-turn access
Install raised median divider with left-turn deceleration lanes
Convert to one-way traffic
Install traffic signals at high-volume driveways
Channelize median openings to prevent left-turns
Widen right through lane or install deceleration lane for right turns
Install channelizing islands to prevent left-turn deceleration lane vehicles from returning to the through lanes
Install barrier to prevent uncontrolled access along property frontages
Install median channelization to control the merge of left-turn out vehicles
Install channelizing island to control the merge area of right-turn out vehicles

Chapter Four

ACCESS MANAGEMENT

Access management is the planning and limitation of access points to street right-of-way. The access points can be public, such as an intersecting street, or private, such as a private driveway. Access limitations vary from a freeway where the only access is from interchanges, down to local streets where every property is allowed a driveway for access. In between freeways and local streets is where it gets sticky.

Freeways and highways are for large volumes of traffic to flow smoothly over long distances, while local streets are to provide access to each property, with traffic moving at lower speeds over short distances. In between are the collector and arterial streets where there is an inherent conflict between the transportation agency's desire to keep traffic flowing safely and quickly, and the property owner's desire for convenient access driveways.

Every driveway leading onto a street creates the risk of accidents, and can slow traffic when vehicles enter or leave. From the perspective of transportation agencies, these are often seen as a bad thing. The convenience (or inconvenience) of access to property is not their first concern, or even their second concern. It is tough for property owners when their concerns start out in third place or lower on the priority list.

Access management is industry jargon for closing or restricting driveways, and the term is often used as a euphemism to sugarcoat the bitter pill. It usually occurs when streets are being widened and traffic increases are expected. Certainly, if the government announces an access management study or plan, you should expect them to try to close as many driveways as feasible. The higher the functional classification, the greater the risk that the study will propose to close all or most driveways.

There are four primary techniques for access management on a commercial street: elimination of private driveways; consolidation of multiple driveways; installation of a median; and realignment of access points.

Elimination of private driveways requires the properties to take access from a side street. If faced with this situation, try to place the side-street access on the downstream side of the property, so that vehicles passing by can see the property well before needing to make the turn. If access is on the upstream side, then drivers must turn before they see the property well, which leads to fewer vehicles making the turn.

Consolidation of multiple access points into one location reduces the number of conflict points, improving traffic flow and safety. The hard part is getting the owners and tenants of the multiple driveways to agree on a plan for doing so.

Medians prevent left turns into most if not all of the private driveways on a commercial street. This can be a disaster for some properties, especially for businesses that rely on rush hour traffic where the flow differs in the morning and afternoon. For example, a breakfast restaurant that is on the opposite side of the street from the morning commute will suffer greatly if those commuters cannot turn left into the restaurant.

The fourth type is realignment of access points, so that driveways on opposite sides of the street are directly across from each other, forming a four-way intersection. Four-way intersections accommodate left turns much more safely than when the driveways are not directly across from each other.

Access management benefits some properties and harms others, and it is important to understand which properties will benefit and which will be harmed. While access management results in closure of driveways, it usually allows upgrades to any that remain open, and upgrades to intersections along the route. The key is to learn which properties are well positioned to utilize an upgraded driveway or intersection, and which are likely to have driveways closed and are poorly positioned to utilize the upgrades.

As a general principle, every property needs a driveway access, with the exceptions being in very urban areas. So, in an access management program, the transportation agency looks for properties with more than one access, especially when one access is from a side street. The preference is to close the driveway on the primary street, so that vehicles can only access the property from the side street. This improves traffic flow on the primary street, because turns then occur at the public street intersection, which is more easily managed, especially when there is a signal.

If all driveways cannot be closed on a block, the number of driveways may be limited by access spacing standards, which are the rules about how far driveways must be from each other and from intersections. For example, in Reno, driveways on major arterials should be 235 feet from intersections, which drops to 150 feet on minor arterials, and 50 feet on collectors. Note that different agencies measure from different points, such as the driveway edge or the center. The same is true for intersections: some measure from the centerline, others from the edge.

The challenge is when the minimum access spacing standard exceeds the width of a property frontage, and thus it is not possible to have an access that meets the spacing standard. In that situation, the transportation agency looks for properties that might be able to share an access, and tries to "consolidate" two or more driveways into one driveway that serves several properties. For example, a new driveway might be placed right at the boundary between properties. This requires easements, which neighboring property owners may or may not be willing to provide.

This brings us to aggregation. Most commercial streets were first developed with numerous smaller lots that were separately owned and operated, each with its own access. That may have sufficed for decades, but as traffic increases smaller frontage lots become less and less practical. Left turns in particular are more difficult, and two-way left turn lanes were tagged with the moniker "suicide lane."

Access management creates winners and losers. The winners are the larger properties that meet the spacing standards and can design driveways, side streets, or signals to comfortably handle their additional traffic. The losers are smaller properties that cannot meet the spacing standards. The smaller properties may be on the corner, where congestion at the intersection obstructs the driveway or forces closure of the driveway on the primary street. Smaller properties mid-block are most at risk of being pressured to share access with a neighbor.

Another risk for smaller properties is that widening of the street may create internal circulation problems. When evaluating property on a commercial street, ask what will happen if another lane or two is added. How hard would it be to pull the front property line back 18 feet, or 24 feet? While it only takes 11 or 12 feet for another traffic lane, chances are good that additional width will be taken for a bike lane, a wider sidewalk, and a landscape strip. This book is not about parking lots and internal circulation, but be aware that some properties can withstand street widening better than others.

Access management usually accompanies a street-widening project. It is crucial to consider what will happen when the street gets wider and the number of access points is reduced, even if a widening project is not imminent. Some properties are well-positioned for this change, and others are not. Properties that are not will suffer severely when the change occurs. If this seems like an exaggeration, attend a public meeting about one of these projects, and listen to the desperation in the voices of the property owners who will be adversely affected.

When streets get widened and driveways close, smaller properties may no longer be viable. The solution to their problem is aggregation; that is, to combine the smaller properties into larger ones. Remember the widened street will bring more vehicles past the property frontage, which only helps if there is a simple access. For a property to benefit from the public investment in a wider street, it needs good access, and some smaller properties on every project simply do not make the cut.

Larger properties may qualify for an access, or may extend from mid-block to the end of the block, and thus have good access to a side street and to the main street via the intersection. They may successfully join forces with their neighbors, by aggregating their properties to a lesser or greater degree. Sharing an access point that straddles a common boundary is the simplest thing. A reciprocal easement with shared parking takes it a step further. Unified ownership is the final step, when smaller property owners sell out to their larger neighbors or create a new entity to own the combined properties.

ACCESS SPACING STANDARDS

There are three basic types of access spacing standards: standards for the distance between public street intersections; standards for the distance between driveways on a street segment; and standards for the distance between driveways and intersections. In addition, each functional classification of street will have one standard for the distance between intersections with streets of the same type, and one standard for the distance between intersections with streets of the next lower classification. For example, large portions of western cities like Las Vegas and Phoenix are laid out on one-mile grids. The major arterials form a grid of mile-wide squares; the standard distance between major arterials is one mile.

Then there will be a standard for the distance between intersections of collector streets and the arterial. Tucson likes to space arterials every one or two miles, and collectors every half-mile. These standards are important because they affect which streets are likely to be upgraded to a higher classification and eventually widened. In order to determine whether a property is well positioned for future changes in access, you must first understand where the street fits into the larger street pattern in the transportation agency's long range plans.

Consider a large undeveloped property at the edge of a growing suburb. It matters immensely both where the agency plans the streets, and what their intended classification will be, during both the short term and the long term. Much money has been squandered on wonderful master plans that were forced to change because they conflict with the access spacing standards and other established plans for the area.

Coordination with neighbors is also essential. Because four way intersections work best, see if your access can be aligned directly across from the neighbor's, and if a signal can be installed there. This often requires many hundred feet of frontage on both sides of the street, but when it works, it works great. The agency is happy because there are no driveways to interfere with traffic on the street, and the signal provides excellent access to the involved properties. Everybody wins.

The second type of access spacing standard is the distance between driveways. The higher the functional classification of the street, the longer the distance will be. Ideally, the frontage width of your property and the location of neighbor driveways will exceed the standard, thus assuring you of an access point.

The third spacing standard is for the distance between driveways and intersections. Obviously this is a huge issue for corner properties. Corner properties are famous for their excellent visibility and access. However, when streets get wider and traffic increases, the access is more difficult to maintain. For our purposes, the point is to check with the right transportation agency official to learn what the standard is, and compare that with the length of the frontage and any existing site conditions.

Existing driveways frequently do not meet one or more spacing standards. When that occurs, you must ascertain the risk that the driveway will need to be moved or closed, and whether the driveway will continue to function well given changing traffic patterns. For example, allowing right turns at red lights improves the operation of driveways approaching the intersection, because traffic flows better in the right lane. However, around the corner, driveways will operate worse because those same vehicles that used to be prevented from turning at a red light now steadily stream past.

The wise man doesn't give the right answers,
he poses the right questions.

Claude Levi-Strauss

CHAPTER FIVE
DUE DILIGENCE

Due diligence is the methodical evaluation of a property being considered for purchase or lease (or if you work for a lender, as security for a loan). To be effective, the evaluation must be diligent, and to be diligent it must analyze five primary aspects of the access. Often, one or more of these aspects is not researched, and often people skate by without difficulty. Other times, it is later discovered that the ice is unexpectedly thin, and the skater falls through. This chapter is about checking the ice.

The five primary aspects of due diligence are: the permit status of existing access, documented access rights and restrictions, the current and prospective government regulations, the functional quality of the existing access, and the likelihood of other traffic changes which could act to the benefit or detriment of the access.

Permits are required for access, and are obtained from the transportation agency (or agencies) responsible for the street right-of-way. The first step is to obtain the permits for any existing access from the transportation agency. The permit will most likely be very specific about the location and width of the access. Check that the actual driveway conforms to the specifications on the permit. If it doesn't, you should figure out why. Perhaps the property was renovated, and the new design was approved by the local government, but they gave you an older access permit instead of the most recent one. Perhaps the access was installed without a permit.

Access rights may be contained in deed documents that are recorded. If so, the title report should include the rights with the legal description of the property. Obtain these documents from the title company and read them carefully. When granting access, many agencies like to place access restrictions (read prohibitions) on the rest of the property frontage. These restrictions can be in deeds or plats, or both, and should appear on the title report as special exceptions. This is a problem if you intend to move the access. These access documents can be confusing, especially for those who are not familiar with plats, legal descriptions, and engineering terminology. It is often necessary to ferret out more documents than are listed in the title report. Be sure to understand what they are saying and to check for consistency among the documents and on the site.

The current regulations can be obtained from the responsible transportation agency. There may be more than one agency and thus more than one layer of regulation. The first thing to check is whether the regulations have changed since any existing access was approved. If the answer is yes, speak with an agency official about the change and determine how it may affect the access. Is the current access grandfathered? If the property is redeveloped, can the same access be used? Can it be widened, signalized, or moved? On larger properties, must one or more access points be consolidated (read closed)? The agency official should have answers to these questions, but if you do not receive a straightforward response, realize the uncertainty is a potential problem. More specific information regarding different types of access rights is in the next chapter.

Agencies plan far ahead, and it's wise to learn about what the future holds before you buy. The agency planning staff is usually separate from the access permitting staff (the exception is smaller jurisdictions), so ask for the person who does long-range planning. Is a long-range plan in place for the property frontage? Has it been implemented? If not, is funding for implementation in the pipeline? How will the implementation affect the access in the short term? How will it affect the access in a long term redevelopment scenario? For example, if a center median is going to be installed, will left turns be prohibited?

To analyze the functional quality of the access, watch how it operates during rush hour, and realize that rush hour may vary based on neighboring land uses. Is traffic backed up entering or leaving the property? Drive in and out on a dark evening, if possible. If there is an alley or service street in the back, drive through at night and on weekends, to see what goes on. Is it comfortable, hair-raising, or something in between?

Check the condition of the pavement and the curbs. If the curbs are in rough shape, chances are the access isn't wide enough for trucks, and their back wheels are running over the curb. If there are scrapes in the pavement, the slope is too severe. If the access is striped, look at the wear spots because that is where people are actually driving. If the wear spots differ much from where the stripes suggest they are supposed to be driving, find out why. Is sun glare an issue? Streets are sloped for drainage, and it's difficult to match the grade at access points, so have a look on a rainy day too. Does water from the property flow into the street or vice versa? Can pedestrians cross safely? Last, but not least, ask tenants, vendors and service providers - if there is a problem, they will know.

Towns evolve and traffic changes. Even in the absence of projects that alter the street, traffic flows can change dramatically when the use of a neighboring property changes or intensifies. For example, if a manufacturing plant adds a second shift, instead of x number of vehicles leaving the plant at 5 p.m., there may be x vehicles entering plus x vehicles exiting the property at 3 p.m. Schools create huge amounts of traffic, and many schools lack the funds to pay for street improvements. Watch what happens at 3 p.m. Perhaps the extra traffic will benefit your property, but if the access is too close to the school, there may be an extended period where it does not operate well. So, look around the neighborhood, and ask whether your access will still function smoothly if more traffic suddenly appears.

The public good is in nothing more essentially interested, than in the protection of every individual's public rights.

Sir William Blackstone

CHAPTER SIX

ACCESS RIGHTS

This chapter reviews common types of access rights. Some access rights, such as abutter's rights and easements, traditionally accrued without formal regulatory approval. Other access rights, especially in recent years, derive from regulatory approvals. Different states and local governments use different terminology, and regulations vary from place to place, but the examples in this chapter are taken from Florida. Especially for older commercial properties, access rights may be less than clear. Some property owners and governments keep better records than others, and when records are available, an experienced local lawyer will be able to explain their meaning. When the records are unavailable, there is research to be done. Since the 1980s, most cities have required permits for access to arterials and state highways. For example, in Florida any access to the state highway that was established after July 1, 1988 requires a permit.

ABUTTER'S RIGHTS

Traditionally, when a public right-of-way was established, all properties abutting the right-of-way had access; these are abutter's rights. This was customary and no permits were required. Then streets were improved, cars became faster, and transportation officials learned that by limiting access, cars could go even faster, and more safely, too. On many new or renovated limited-access streets such as arterials and freeways, the transportation agency purchases the real estate for the right-of-way and also expressly purchases the abutter's right of access. For streets being widened, the government similarly purchases access rights for most if not all of the property frontage. Nevertheless, the concept of abutter's rights is still in effect, with the caveat being that while every property (theoretically) is entitled to have access to a public street, every property is not entitled to access to every street. Thus, a property with frontage on a busy arterial may be compelled to take access from a lower classification side street or back street. Nor is a property entitled to access at any desired location on a street.

EASEMENT RIGHTS

One property may have an easement across another for access to a right-of-way, which is not the same thing as saying the easement holder has the right to access the right-of-way. The easement holder will still need to comply with the applicable access regulations. Often private easements for commercial property are reciprocal, so that each property has access rights across the other. This allows properties in separate ownership to function as one property, at least for access purposes. Easement rights are a source of much confusion and angst. If you are interested in a property that relies on an easement for access, gather all the pertinent documents and take them to a local real estate lawyer.

Access rights can also be lost if they are not used. For example, if a private access easement is not used, it may be deemed abandoned and terminated. In addition, some private easements provide that the owner of the property that the easement crosses has the right to relocate the easement at their own expense.

WAY OF NECESSITY

Landlocked property is a hardship and government officials strive to prevent creation of new ones. Unfortunately, landlocked property is still out there and a "way of necessity" is one method for providing access. For example, Florida recognizes two types: an implied grant and a statutory right. The implied grant of a way of necessity occurs when person A sells property to person B that would otherwise be landlocked - the law grants B a way of necessity over A's property to reach a right-of-way. This only works where A's property abuts both the property being sold and the right-of-way. The statutory right takes effect when no practical access route is present even though the owner has vested easement rights, and is in addition to the easement rights.

LOSS OF ACCESS RIGHTS

Most transportation agencies attach conditions to access rights they grant. The conditions may include a cap on the amount of traffic that uses an access. For example, an access permit for an apartment complex onto an arterial may state that the permit is for residential use only. Failure to comply with the conditions of a permit may cause the access rights to be lost, notably when a traffic accident occurs and investigation reveals that use of the access is not in compliance with the conditions.

Now fast forward a few decades and assume the tired apartments are ripe for redevelopment into a shopping center. The transportation agency, being mindful that shopping centers generate much more traffic than apartments, expects to review the plans for the shopping center and reconsider the prior access permit. Perhaps the old driveway will still work, but chances are it will need to be widened at a minimum, and possibly (or likely) relocated to a side street. This scenario is known as a change in use, and most sophisticated jurisdictions will have numerical standards to specify when a valid permit must be reevaluated. For access permits to Florida State Highways, the triggers for reevaluation are any change that increases trip generation (either daily or during the peak hour) on the property more than 25 percent, or any change that increases trip generation by more than 100 vehicles per day.

Access rights may be of limited duration, and may sunset after a certain number of years, or when an alternate access becomes available. For example, imagine the street is being widened and the transportation agency wants to close an access, but the property lacks alternative access. If there is another project in the pipeline that could provide alternate access in the future, the agency will likely insert a sunset clause in the permit to terminate and close the original access when the alternate access becomes operational.

If an access causes safety problems, the transportation agency may take action, even against a permitted access. The agency may insist on improvements, such as installation of a median to prohibit left turns. It may compel a property owner to relocate the access, or even close it in extreme cases. Again using the Florida State Highways as our example, the authority to "take immediate remedial action" is held by the seven District Secretaries (of the Florida Department of Transportation).

SALE OF ACCESS RIGHTS

Transportation agencies purchase access rights all the time, the obvious example being for a new freeway where, as noted above, the purchase documents will include the right of access. For a street widening project, agencies often purchase access rights for the entire frontage of a property when possible, and if not, they purchase access rights for almost the entire frontage, except for the access point(s). When a transportation agency purchases partial access rights, the deed and exhibits should specify the location(s) where access is permitted; the generic term for this is deeded access.

MAXIMUM VOLUME TO CAPACITY RATIOS			
	Non-freeway posted speed <= 35mph, or a designated UBA	Non-freeway speed > 35 mph	Non-freeway speed limit >= 45mph
Interstate Highways	n/a	0.70	0.70
Statewide Expressways	0.70	0.70	0.70
Freight Route on a Statewide Highway	0.80	0.75	0.70
Statewide (not a Freight Route)	0.85	0.80	0.75
Freight Route on a Regional or District Highway	0.85	0.80	0.75
Expressway on a Regional or District Highway	n/a	0.80	0.75
Regional Highways	0.85	0.80	0.75
District / Local Interest Roads	0.90	0.85	0.80

CHAPTER SEVEN
A PRIMER ON TRAFFIC STUDIES

A traffic study is the report written by a transportation engineer to analyze traffic within the parameters established by the responsible transportation agency (or agencies) that determines the scope of the study. The two basic types are government studies to analyze the public street system for a land use plan or a public works project, and private studies to analyze how a proposed development will affect the surrounding streets and highways.

STUDIES FOR GOVERNMENT PROJECTS

Government studies typically examine a street and its intersections in anticipation of widening the street and are sometimes called corridor studies. Of particular importance to property owners, the studies examine access along the corridor, and often strive to close as many driveways as possible. Close attention is also paid to the beginning and end points of the project, where it must connect with an existing or future street.

As government studies, political influences should be kept in mind when analyzing their assumptions, data and conclusions. To be thorough, try to speak with the engineer who did the legwork or wrote the first draft, and you may learn useful information that was deleted in the final report.

Modernization projects facilitate increases in traffic, for which extensive studies are standard. These projects include safety improvements as well, such as straightening dangerous curves and adding turn lanes. Projects which just resurface the street that is already there are called preservation, and usually do not require studies, except perhaps analysis of traffic control and detours during the construction period.

The government agencies that manage streets and highways keep transportation engineers on staff. However, when contemplating a new project, the agency usually hires out the engineering work, including the traffic analysis, to a private firm. Most of the time, the project goal is to move more vehicles faster and more safely. In some jurisdictions, the goal is to manage (read impede) vehicular traffic in order to promote other modes of transportation, such as bikes and transit.

STUDIES FOR LAND DEVELOPMENT PROJECTS

When land is being planned for development, the goal is for the surrounding street network to function well after the project is complete and fully occupied. In most projects, the developer seeks to minimize the cost of street improvements, at the risk of slowing traffic. The transportation agency naturally seeks to maximize the amount of street improvements it can compel the development to construct at its own expense. The risk is that excessive demands for public improvements will kill a project and the benefits, such as increased tax revenue, that would accrue.

THE SCOPE OF THE TRAFFIC STUDY

This delicate negotiation begins with defining the scope for the traffic study. Each street segment, intersection or interchange to be studied increases the cost of the study, and increases the likelihood that the study will discover problems that must be dealt with, usually at the developer's expense. Since the development pays for the study, the transportation agency has the incentive to broaden the study in order to learn more about their streets. The study is done by a private traffic engineer hired by the developer, in accordance with the scope of work agreed to with the transportation agency. Note that some agencies insist that developers hire a particular engineer.

The particulars of the scope are somewhat discretionary and may be adjusted. The narrower the scope, the less expensive the study, but if the scope is too narrow, the study is subject to challenge by project opponents. The scope begins with the geographic area being considered. For a public works project, this is usually a linear corridor, while for a development project, this is an area around the proposed site. The scope will specify which streets and intersections within this geographic area need to be analyzed, and what the analysis must include.

EXISTING CONDITIONS

The analysis begins with current vehicle trip counts. With the advent of automated counting devices, the cost of vehicle trip counts is modest. You might think that the transportation agency should already know what the current traffic is. If there is a recent study, you may be able to use that data to save the expense of another count. But the transportation agency likes new counts, since they get useful data for free, even if the project never gets built.

A vehicle passing by is called a "vehicle trip" or "trip" for short. ADT means average daily trips, meaning the average number of vehicles passing a particular point on the street over a 24-hour period, and includes vehicles going in both directions. So a report that says Main St. has 4,500 ADTs means that roughly half are going each direction. (Freeway counts are usually reported separately for each direction.)

To avoid anomalous traffic conditions, trip counts should be done on Tuesdays, Wednesdays, or Thursdays during weeks without a holiday. The weather should be clear. Counts should be obtained in the morning and afternoon peak hours, and sometimes a Saturday peak hour count will be required. Lastly, watch out for seasonal issues like tourist attractions, and outliers like sporting events that might skew the counts. For example, in a resort town, the trip counts should be taken during the peak season. In a retail area, there should be Saturday counts. Doing the counts at inappropriate times can skew the data.

ESTIMATED TRIP COUNTS AFTER THE PROJECT IS COMPLETE

The next element of the analysis is estimating the additional traffic that will be caused by the proposed project. The anticipated traffic from development projects which are approved, but not yet complete (meaning occupied), are also added.

For public works projects, the question is how much latent demand is out there, meaning how many additional vehicles will happily use the street once it is improved, by widening, for example. Since public works modernization projects usually increase capacity and safety, more vehicles will likely use the street.

For development projects, the issue is the number of vehicles that will come to the site, known as trip generation. Estimating trip generation is a huge issue. Fortunately, the Institute for Traffic Engineers publishes a standard reference book on this topic, known as the ITE Manual, which lists numerous land uses, and presents trip generation data for them based on standard metrics such as building square footage. In most cases, you can simply look up the trip generation rates in the manual. The hard part is when a speculative development is uncertain precisely how much of which land use type(s) will occupy the completed project. For example, a shopping center pad site could be occupied by a branch bank, or by a fast food restaurant which generates more trips and at different times of the day. For redevelopment projects, the trip generation for the prior use is deducted from the new use, which provides the net increase or decrease in trips.

A second issue for development projects is the percentage of trips that will come to the site, but which are already on the street, known as pass-by trips. Fast food restaurants are a good example. The vehicles already on the street for other purposes that simply pull in for a meal really do not increase the number of vehicles on the street, and thus the number of pass-by trips is deducted from the trip generation rate.

TRAFFIC ASSIGNMENT (AKA TRIP DISTRIBUTION)

Once the number of trips generated by the project is estimated, the various routes are forecast, which is known as traffic assignment or trip distribution. The traffic engineer draws a map with the project site in the middle, showing the numbers of vehicles arriving and leaving in every direction, including the number of vehicles turning at all intersections being studied. Trip distribution informs the placement and design of the access points. Traffic studies typically will not separately consider truck access routes, though they will often differ from the routes used by passenger vehicles.

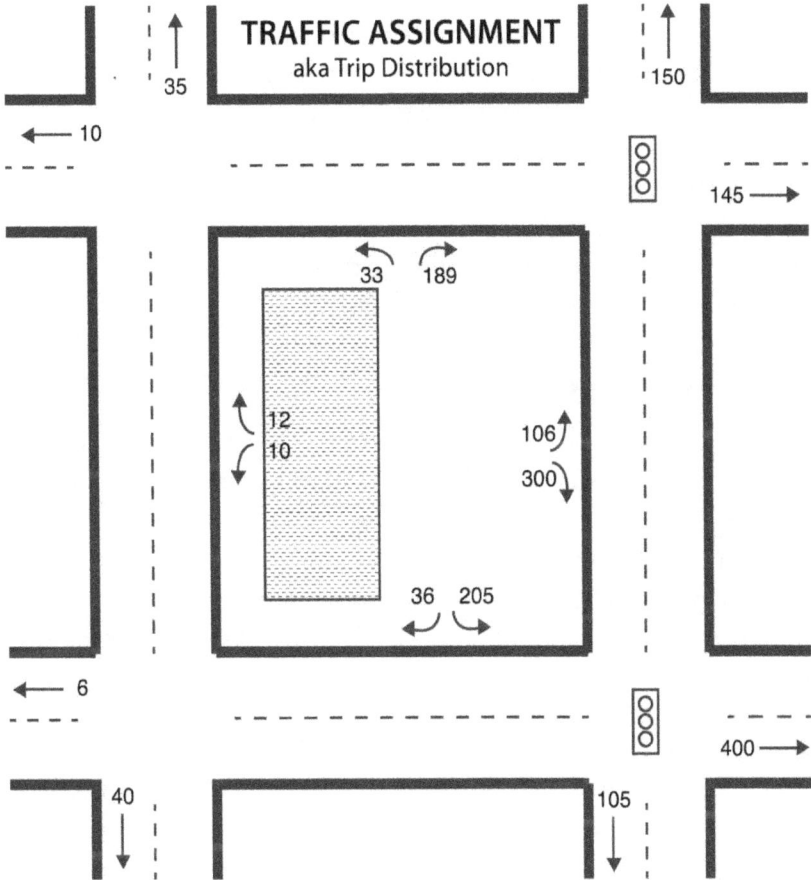

TRAFFIC ASSIGNMENT
aka Trip Distribution

ANALYZING CAPACITY

The next step is to analyze the effect of the new trips on the street system, especially the intersections and any nearby freeway interchanges. The intersection capacity is carefully measured, usually following the methodology in the Highway Capacity Manual 2000 published by the Transportation Research Board (a federal government entity). Each lane and turning movement of the intersection is analyzed separately. If the capacity standards are exceeded, developers are expected to improve the intersection(s) with items such as new lanes, a left-turn lane (or two), longer storage for the left-turn lane(s), or perhaps upgrading of a four-way stop sign to a roundabout. Intersections are expensive, and for most traffic studies intersection capacity is the key thing.

Private developers carefully consider what the transportation agency requires, how much it costs, and whether the requirements seem fair, or whether they seem more related to the agency's project wish list than the needs and impacts of the development. Requirements such as street widening and new signals along the frontage of a shopping center will benefit the property for years to come; a requirement for a new signal around the corner, not so much. Be prepared to work closely with your traffic engineer and negotiate with the transportation agency over the results of the traffic study and the required improvements.

TRAFFIC SIGNALS

Traffic studies count trips and analyze congestion at intersections, which drives the design of traffic lanes and turn signals. We've all experienced signals where the line of vehicles waiting to turn is so long that traffic in the through lane is backed up. A waiting line of vehicles is called a queue. The length of the left-turn lane itself is called the storage length.

Traffic studies demonstrate the need for left-turn capacity, meaning how many left turns the intersection should accommodate. Capacity in turn drives the street design, in terms of storage length and the number of left turn lanes. Capacity is closely related to signal timing, meaning how long the various signals at the intersection are green, yellow and red. Signal timing is controlled by computers in a metal cabinet located at one of the intersection corners which have two basic inputs: the original plan for signal timing, and real-time data from actual traffic on the street.

Real-time data is gathered by signal loops, which are metal detectors embedded in the pavement in the lanes approaching the intersection that tell the controller about the vehicles on the street in real time. They are called loops because they are round, and if you look carefully they are visible (or at least the black seals over them are). Basically, the signals are programmed so if a certain number of vehicles passes, the signal timing is adjusted. For example, if only one or two vehicles is waiting to turn left, the signal may make them wait until the through traffic has passed by the intersection, but if three or more vehicles are waiting to turn the left-turn signal may go green sooner. This is called signal priority.

Once new signals are installed in an intersection, the traffic doesn't always respond as predicted. With fine tuning of the signal priority and timing, unexpected traffic patterns can often be adjusted for with changes to the signal programming. When you see a group of engineering types standing around an open signal cabinet soon after an intersection was rebuilt, they are likely adjusting the programming.

FUTURE PLANNING

Lastly, traffic studies look far into the future, usually at least 20 years. This allows for the long term planning that is necessary for public facilities, since it doesn't make sense to build a street improvement that will only alleviate a traffic problem for a few years. It is much better to overbuild it now, given future increases in traffic, so that it functions smoothly for decades to come. Many jurisdictions have some form of a "latecomer" ordinance, which allows a developer who builds more capacity than is required by their project to be paid back by neighbors for that extra capacity in the future.

Especially for public works projects, future planning raises the issue of induced demand. While latent demand is the number of vehicles already on the street that will shift routes to use a new or improved street, induced demand considers whether the new or improved street will encourage future real estate development that will in turn generate more traffic. Think of how the West was settled: the government subsidized railroads, and then towns grew up around the railroad stations. There was no demand for real estate until the railroad stations were built; that is the railroads induced demand. For potential new streets, the concept is that building them encourages more development.

Another element of long-range planning is the estimated increase in traffic due to population growth. This is usually expressed as a small annual percentage increase. For public works, the larger the project, the longer the expected life span, and the more future traffic must be accounted for. Bridges are the best example because they cannot be widened easily. If the bridge is intended for 75 years of service, many highway engineers recommend designing it to handle traffic increases over that time period.

Design is a funny word. Some people think design means how it looks. But of course, if you dig deeper, it's really how it works.

Steve Jobs

CHAPTER EIGHT

DRIVEWAY DESIGN

Existing driveways sometimes get remodeled, and new ones get built. While most of this book is about where to put the access, this chapter describes how to shape it. The goal is for you to understand the elements of access design to facilitate communication with the civil engineer(s) and negotiation with the responsible transportation agency.

Before we get ahead of ourselves, realize that the agency is likely to have a standard design they expect you to comply with. It will be relatively straightforward, and if the street is straight and flat, you can likely use it without modification, saving the cost of a custom design. If your project is something different, say, if the terrain is sloped, and the standard design is not a good fit, you or your civil engineer will need to negotiate the alterations with the government. This is doable, provided that what you are asking for is genuinely justified by the project.

If your project is a new development larger than 10 acres, there may be major changes required to the street frontage such as changes in the functional classification of the street, the number of lanes, the grade, the sidewalk width and location (curb tight or behind a planter strip), and the speed limit. Otherwise, those items should be included in the design assumptions, and the design must reflect them.

Elements that you may be able to custom design include the lighting, signage, landscaping, entry width, the number and functions of lanes, traffic signals, the corner radius, the curb treatment (meaning the curb and any necessary breaks or slopes), a right-turn deceleration lane for entering the property, and possibly a right-turn acceleration lane for exiting as well.

VISIBILITY

Remember the intention is to make entering and leaving the property as convenient and safe as possible for vehicles, while allowing traffic to flow smoothly on the public street. Good visibility is essential. The four things most likely to obstruct visibility around the driveway are: sign clutter, utility equipment, landscaping, and on-street parking.

Signs may be public or private. We'll start with public traffic signs in the right-of-way. Look carefully, and ask if any of the signs can be moved further away (either upstream or downstream) from the driveway, or removed altogether. If it's been years since the street received much attention, one or more of the signs may be obsolete. If the traffic signs must stay, but are showing their age, acknowledge that old and faded traffic signs can also make commercial property feel old and faded. Curb appeal means everything behind the curb should look sharp, so consider replacing signs at your cost to give the property a fresh look. This may also earn you some goodwill with the agency staff handling the access.

Private sign clutter is usually caused by a proliferation of temporary tenant signs that distract attention in addition to blocking sight lines. For permanent signage, there is an inherent tension between placing the sign close to the driveway and visibility. This is part of why old-school pole signs were popular. Monument signs may be more aesthetically pleasing to modern eyes, however, they can also obstruct views, including views of driveway entrances when poorly placed.

Moving utility equipment, even just a few feet, is very expensive. On larger development projects, most of the utilities will be placed underground, and you only need to watch the location of light poles and utility cabinets, such as pad-mounted transformers. Most developers prefer to screen the cabinets with shrubs, or put them underground as well, so be sure to get the electric company especially, and also the gas company and the phone company, in the loop early on.

Signalized driveways need one or more signal cabinets. Insist that they be placed on the downstream side of the intersection where it will not obstruct the views of entering or exiting vehicles. (Or better yet, across the street.) Other public utilities and equipment that can clutter or obstruct views are fire hydrants, and bus stop shelters, and traffic signal poles. Bus stops also cause congestion when buses are present, by obstructing views and vehicles trying to use an access adjacent to buses which are slowing, stopped, or accelerating. If they must be along the street frontage, move them downstream of the driveway when possible, and back from the curb when not.

For landscaping, select slender street trees, and be sure to regularly remove lower limbs up to a height of at least six feet. Watch the selection of shrubs and groundcovers to ensure they won't get too tall. For visibility, nothing beats grass.

On-street parking is tougher. Where it exists, every space is likely considered precious. Make sure the space on the upstream side of the driveway is back far enough – and the farther the better – to allow easy right turns into the driveway. Likewise, make sure the first downstream space allows easy right turns out. Perhaps shifting the driveway location a few feet or presenting a wider driveway design might help.

Lastly, instruct the civil engineer to inform you about any miscellaneous items that attempt to sneak into the later stages of a street design. As your project gathers momentum within the various public agencies and utilities, the Christmas tree effect can occur, where everyone feels compelled to add something (usually at your cost), and a clean design becomes cluttered. Ideally, vehicles approaching the driveway will primarily see your private sign and the driveway itself, but it's not a perfect world, so be prepared to work hard on these items to make the visibility the best it can be.

CURB CUTS

The next topic is the various types of curb treatments, known as curb cuts. Most small and midsize properties have drop down or dustpan curbs as shown below.

DROP DOWN CURB

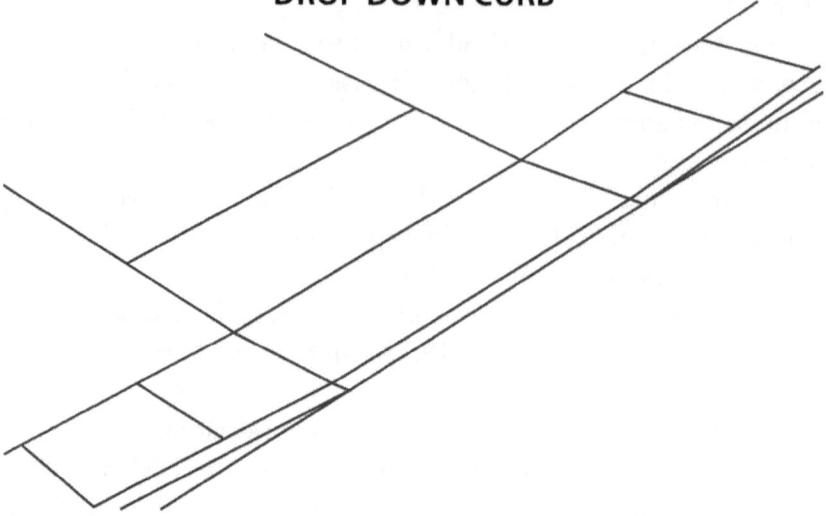

DUST PAN CURB

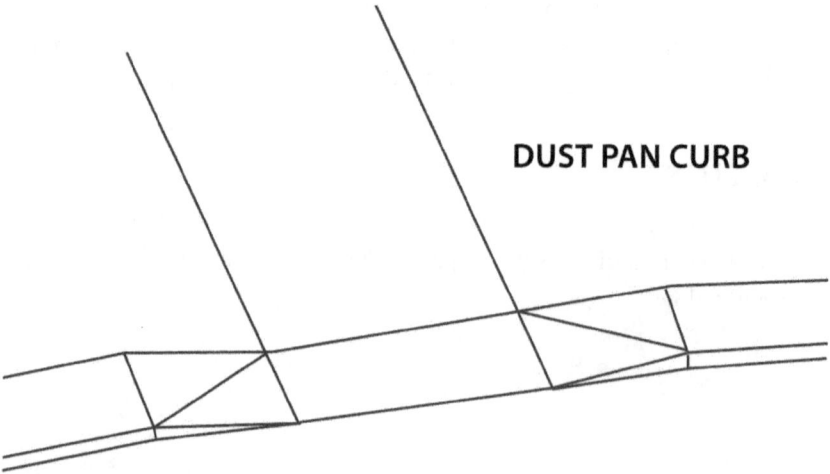

In the dust pan type, the top of the curb remains level and the bottom slants up along with the driveway pavement to a point where the curb disappears.

An upgrade common on larger projects is a curb return, as shown below. Note how the curb is not linear, but rather curves into the property to form the edge of the driveway.

CURB RADIUS

4.6m (15') R

7.5m (25') R

15.2m (50') R

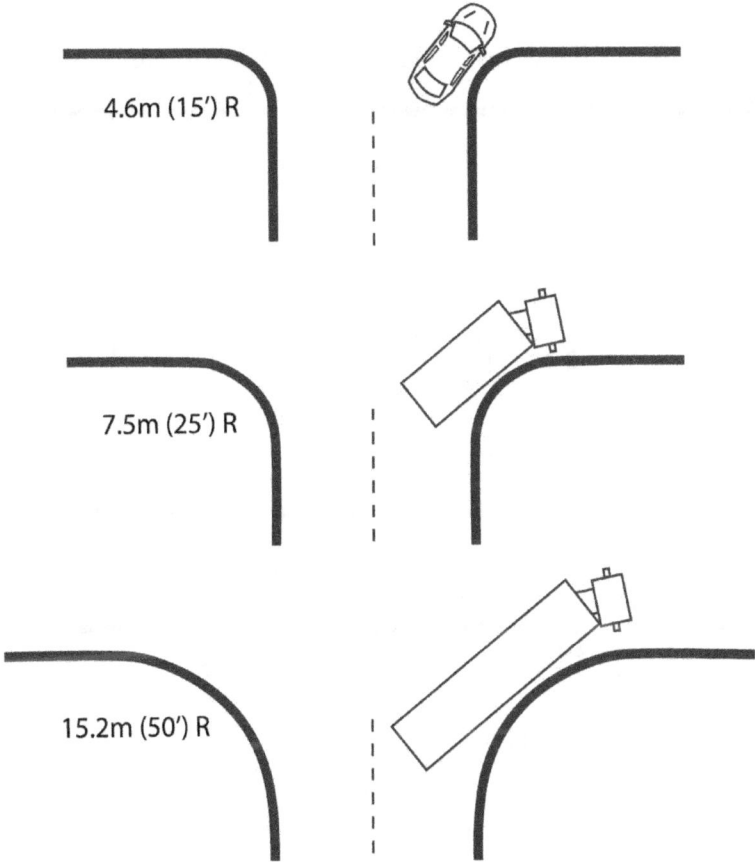

A larger radius makes a wider curve, known as the arc. In contrast to the flare type, the height of the radius curb return stays the same. This feature makes the driveway more visible, and it appears more like a street intersection. The radius will increase with more traffic, higher speeds, and larger vehicles. For the largest properties, the radius can range up to 50 feet along a high-speed arterial and down to 25 feet for local streets. Small-scale commercial driveways can get by with a radius of 15 or 20 feet, though larger ones are more comfortable. Also, trucks need a large radius.

Radius curb returns reduce the lineal footage of straight curb available for on-street parking.

A radius curb return is more difficult to build, in part because the sidewalk crossing becomes a challenge. Typically the sidewalk is moved deeper into the property where the radius curve ends.

WHEN THE RADIUS IS TOO SMALL

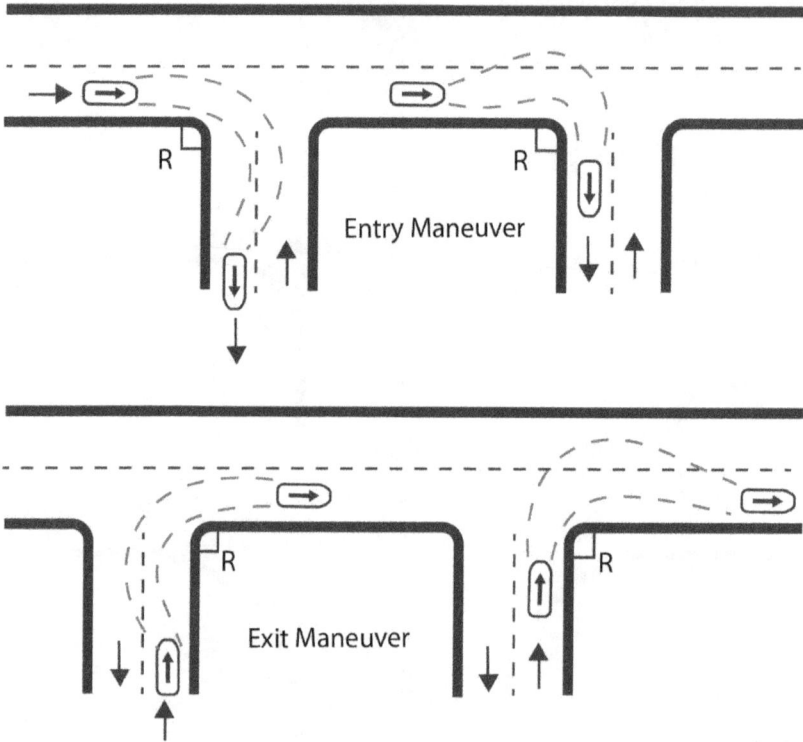

Entry Maneuver

Exit Maneuver

CHANNELIZATION

Next we'll review where the middle of the driveway meets the street. Most commercial driveways function well without anything there, but some two-lane driveways and almost all driveways of three or more lanes divide the traffic into lanes, called channelization. Options include striping, and islands of two basic types: medians and pork chops.

When a driveway is restricted to only right-in and right-out turns, some naughty and reckless drivers will attempt to make the prohibited left turns, unless a little friendly persuasion is provided. This usually takes the form of a small raised island in a generally triangular shape, known as a pork chop, which effectively blocks most left turns, except for rambunctious four-wheelers. Try to paint the curb or otherwise make the outline of the pork chop visible. Vertical elements within a pork chop are discouraged because they obstruct views. Pork chops are very rarely landscaped, in part because it's not cost effective to run irrigation to them for such a small space.

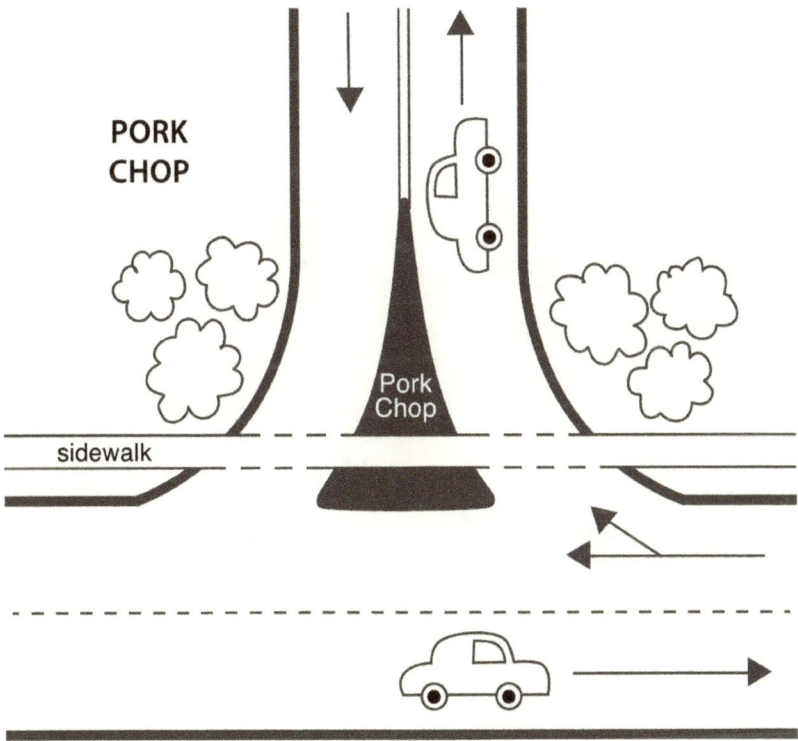

Sometimes a two-lane driveway is not sufficient. Think about trying to turn out of a driveway. You look toward the left, and another car is turning into the same driveway you want to pull out of. The closer the entering vehicle is to yours, the closer the left front bumper of the entering vehicle is to your door. You know the uncomfortable feeling when the entering vehicle is too close, and that bumper is swooping right toward you. The usual upgrade is to widen the driveway a bit.

The next step up is to add a second exit lane dedicated to vehicles turning right. This way, a vehicle waiting to turn left does not block vehicles exiting to the right. Many driveways begin with two lanes at the back of the throat and widen to three lanes where the driveway meets the street. Most three-lane driveway entrances are striped.

For large projects with four or more lanes, the width of the driveway opening combined with the number of vehicles entering and exiting encourages many developers to install a median in the driveway. Because of all the turning movements, the end of the median is often curved in the shape of a bullet head, and that is what they are called.

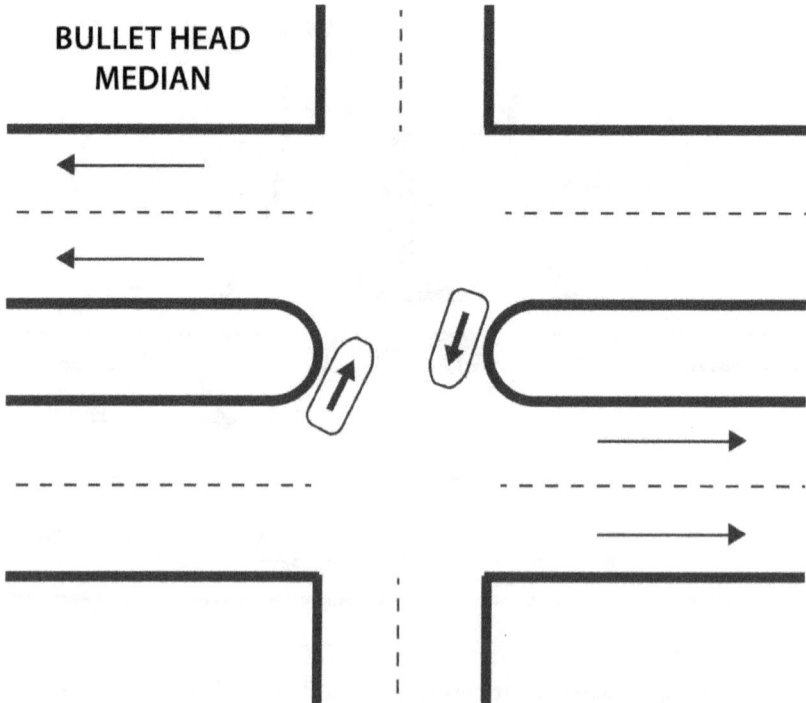

BULLET HEAD
MEDIAN

For a large number of left-turns in only one direction a half-bullet shape is used, as with a three-way intersection.

HALF BULLET MEDIAN

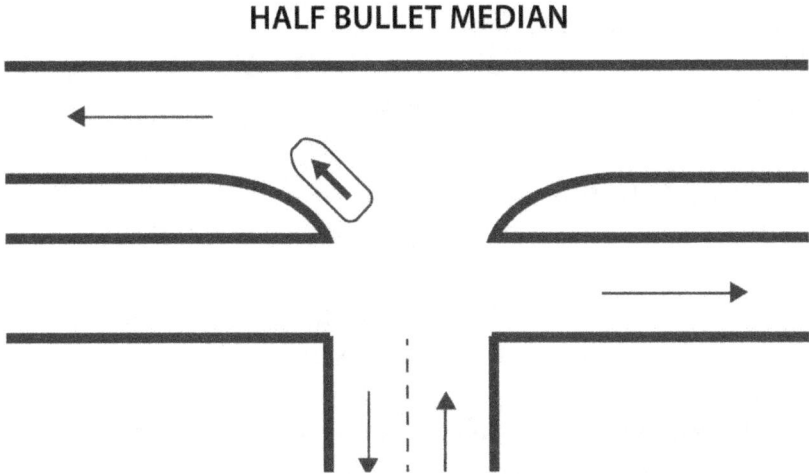

Medians come in different widths, depending on the availability of real estate, the need to channelize traffic, the landscaping design for the entrance, and the need for a pedestrian refuge, among other factors. The central concept of this book is that a simple access is relaxing and good for business. Medians simplify by separating the entering and exiting traffic, so entering drivers need not pay attention to vehicles leaving, and vice versa.

Most medians are at least four feet wide, but they can shrink to two feet wide in a pinch. Medians may narrow as they get closer to the street in order to accommodate additional lanes for exiting vehicles. Medians with a pedestrian refuge should be six feet wide. The median should continue into the property for the full length of the throat, and use bullet heads at the end to accommodate turning.

Landscaping in the median should include low shrubs for a visual buffer and to reduce headlight glare. For properties such as a corporate campus where visibility from the street to building facades is not a priority, the median landscaping can be tall, but for retail, the shrubs should of course, be kept low.

DRAINAGE

Driveways must be checked for stormwater drainage. The pavement and curbs must be sloped enough to prevent puddles and allow the stormwater to flow away. This sounds simple enough, but in practice can be difficult. Look carefully at the existing streets, curbs and catch basins, both on the public street and the private property. Of course visit the site on a rainy day. Moving catch basins, or changing the grade of a public street, are expensive and most people try to avoid them at all costs.

VERTICAL CURVES

When the driveway is lower than the street, this creates a hump in the pavement where the driveway meets the street, also known as a vertical curve or vertical grade. These humps create the risk that vehicles, especially sports cars that are low to the ground, will scrape on the pavement when entering or leaving. (Trailer tongues will scrape as well.) The street pavement is usually graded to prevent stormwater from flowing down the driveway; in other words, it is sloped up precisely at the edge of the street. Lowering the street level is usually not an option. The best solution is for the driveway level to be raised high enough to prevent this problem, however, this makes the driveway steeper further away from the street. Work closely with the civil engineers and contractors to ensure the driveway is high enough to prevent this problem, and recognize that solutions will be expensive.

Aside from the practical need to solve this problem, realize that properties which sit lower than the street suffer from poor visibility, so passing vehicles are likely to brake more abruptly when approaching the driveway.

Where the driveway is higher, and slopes down to meet the street, this creates a valley where the two meet which is called a sag grade. The risk of a sag grade is that the front or rear of vehicles will scrape the pavement. A lesser problem is that stormwater can flow from the driveway onto the street. Lowering the driveway near the street is the best solution, which makes the driveway steeper further back from the street.

PEDS AND BIKES

Driveway designs also must accommodate pedestrians and bicyclists, which really don't mix well with cars traveling more than about 10 miles per hour. According to the National Highway Traffic Safety Administration (Traffic Safety Facts), in 2009, 630 bicyclists died on US roads in (down from 1003 in 1975, the pre-helmet days), and 51,000 bicyclists were injured in traffic. For pedestrians, the majority of accidents involving cars occur on weekend evenings, and not at intersections. So pay special attention if your property or neighbors include nightlife. About 5000 pedestrians are struck and killed by motor vehicles each year.

The best practice is to separate pedestrians and bicyclists from moving vehicles whenever possible. Of course that is impossible where driveways cross sidewalks and meet the street. Many transportation agencies insist on better facilities for pedestrians and bicyclists both on public streets and within private properties. This necessity can become a virtue if the facilities also benefit those traveling by car or truck. For safety's sake, pedestrian and bike facilities should have good sightlines. Try to place these sightlines in a way that supplements the sightlines serving vehicles.

Second, bike lanes are often required in the street along the property frontage. Near driveways, the extra road width provided by a bike lane provides space for vehicles slowing to turn right into a driveway. This extra width reduces stress for drivers, and the number of rear-end collisions, and is especially beneficial for truck turns. Of course this is only true when there are no bicycles in the bike lane.

Yes, expanded pedestrian and bike facilities will consume valuable real estate, and yes, they may not be cost effective in suburban areas where few people use them. That does not mean that you won't need to provide them. When evaluating property frontage, determine whether the existing facilities are up to the current standards, whether the standards are being increased. And don't be surprised if they increase in the future. Always ask yourself how the frontage would be reconfigured to accommodate expanded pedestrian and bike facilities.

The only man who behaves sensibly is my tailor; he takes my measurements anew every time he sees me, while all the rest go on with their old measurements and expect me to fit them.

George Barnard Shaw

PART 2 – ACCESS FOR LAND USES

The real estate industry includes a variety of sectors which operate differently in order to serve their respective functions, and they require different types of access. To give but one example, a hospital needs an ambulance entrance that is set well away from other access that could become congested and delay the delivery of patients to the emergency room.

Broadly speaking, there are residential, retail, office, mixed use, industrial, public and institutional properties, and they vary in scale dramatically. Yet with few exceptions each of these properties has vehicle access. Ideally, the access location and design are tailored to the particular land use. However, the access regulations are driven by the street classification, not individual land uses, and agency staff will expect your access to fit their rules.

For top performing real estate, especially for auto dependent land uses, it is essential that the access fit the site design, and not vice versa. Part 2 describes how to make it so.

TABLE OF DRIVEWAY WIDTHS
For Smaller Properties

Land Use	Peak Hour Volume	Style	Throat Width
Single Family	0-10	Dust Pan	16'
Single Family	11+	Dust Pan	24'
Multi-Family	0-10	Dust Pan	16'
Multi-Family	11-150	Dust Pan	24'-28'
Multi-Family	151-300	Dust Pan	36'-40'
Multi-Family	301-399	Radius	Variable
Multi-Family	400+	Radius	Variable
Commercial	0-20	Dust Pan	24'
Commercial	21-150	Dust Pan	28'-32'
Commercial	151-300	Dust Pan	36'-46'
Commercial	301-399	Radius	Variable
Commercial	400+	Radius	Variable
Industrial		Dust Pan / Radius	Variable
Industrial		Radius	Variable

CHAPTER NINE

SINGLE FAMILY RESIDENTIAL

The typical single-family house is served by a typical driveway, and you might be thinking there isn't much to vehicle access for a single-family property, and you're right. But the real estate professional involved with creating or evaluating single-family neighborhoods is compelled to consider access to the neighborhood as a whole, given that each lot will usually have its own driveway.

Besides, this chapter will help you understand what's going on around your own house. Vehicle circulation within the neighborhood is of keen interest, especially to parents. The leading types of street patterns are the grid, the loop, and the cul-de-sac.

THE GRID

The grid is just that – a rectangular system of streets, with each block having roughly eight to sixteen lots, and each lot having its own driveway. The idea behind the street grid is what planners call connectivity. In a grid system anyone can drive anywhere fairly directly, reducing "out-of-direction travel" which is especially important for pedestrians and bicyclists.

The grid provides numerous route choices, which is very helpful in the event of traffic jams, street construction, and the like. The catch is that grids also allow traffic to cut through single-family neighborhoods. Watch out for apparently quiet residential streets that are parallel to larger streets, or that lead to a busy local destination, such as a school or church. Before you buy, visit the block during the rush hour, or better yet ask someone in the neighborhood if this is an issue.

Developers usually place the driveway to one side of the lot, and some prefer that the driveways on adjacent lots be next to each other, the idea being that the cars are together and one person's cars are not next to another person's living room window. This also simplifies installation of underground dry utilities (which are often placed between the driveways).

The grid pattern is often frowned upon by developers because it consumes more real estate for the streets and costs more to build than other patterns. This can be compensated for with longer blocks in some jurisdictions.

THE LOOP

The loop is a pattern with curved streets instead of straight ones. The exception is street intersections, which are made as close to perpendicular as possible. Looped streets are often considered more visually attractive because when looking straight ahead, drivers and passengers see more yards and houses, as compared with a straight street where the view is of more pavement.

The driver can only see as far ahead as the curve permits. The sharper the curve, the less of the street ahead can be seen. The curve also affects how far drivers entering the street from a driveway can see oncoming traffic, known as "sight distance." Sight distance is also limited by obstacles such as shrubbery, fences, and parked cars. In a single-family neighborhood, the speed limit should be low enough that a relatively short sight distance does not pose a safety hazard. To address the hazard, most jurisdictions prohibit visual obstacles taller than 30 inches in a triangular area where a driveway meets the street and where streets intersect. This area is called the "sight triangle." The higher the speed limit, the larger the triangle needs to be. You might ask what benefit is provided by a clear sight triangle on the private property if parking is allowed on the street. The simple answer is not much, and if parked cars obscure views, extra caution must be exercised. On-street parking often obstructs views in older residential neighborhoods, especially in the evenings and overnight.

THE CUL-DE-SAC

Cul-de-sacs are the modern form of dead-end streets. Cul-de-sacs simply allow vehicles approaching the end of the street to turn around. They can be placed within either grid or loop street systems; however, jurisdictions which favor the grid usually prohibit or severely limit cul-de-sacs. There are two primary issues: the size of the circle at the end of the street, and the consequences of a dead end street.

Modern cul-de-sacs usually end in a circle, and the first question facing a developer is the size of that circle, described as the radius. Recognize there are two edges to think about: the curb and also the right-of-way line (usually at or near the back of the sidewalk). Whenever discussing the required radius, determine whether it extends to the curb or to the right-of-way line. While the traffic engineers (and the local fire department) will ensure the radius is large enough for vehicles to negotiate the circle, they won't be as concerned about how wide the sidewalk is, or whether the sidewalk will be separated from the street by a planting strip. Well-written engineering standards will specify both the minimum radius to the curb, and also the additional radius required for the broader right-of-way.

The lots facing onto the circle will be pie shaped, and if the radius is too small, the fronts of the lots will be awkwardly narrow. If the radius is too large, the circular paved area becomes larger and can be a huge waste of real estate. Many developers make this necessity into a virtue by enlarging the radius so that the center of the circle can be put to productive use, such as landscaping (think roundabout) or parking. Another benefit of larger circles is that they provide wider lot frontages.

Dead-end streets are preferred by many families because the traffic is very light and moves very slowly. This is ideal for children playing, and general peace and quiet. The flip side is that from the perspective of many transportation officials, dead end streets are a headache. Since these quiet streets are used for so many activities, neighbors pay closer attention to them, which results in numerous complaints to public officials about items such as basketball hoops. And, when street repairs become necessary, the jurisdiction does not get much value because, while the cost is the same as for any other local street, dead-end streets do not carry much traffic.

THE TROPHY HOUSE

Houses of a larger scale require more of everything, including access, circulation and parking. In recent times, larger houses, say 5000 square feet and up, have sprouted on lots and blocks that are no larger than those created for modest size homes. In that circumstance, the access is similar to other single family properties.

Ideally a larger-scale home will be sited on a larger lot which affords extra room for vehicles and their various needs. The scale of the garage is usually proportionally large, and ideally, the garage will be placed some distance from the main entry. Nevertheless, vehicles should be able to pull up to, or at least close to, the main entry. The result is often a broad paved area which can feel inappropriate if it isn't managed carefully. Options include mobile landscaping, such as potted plants that can be relocated as necessary, and basketball hoops.

Vehicles should also have direct access to a side entrance, usually placed near the kitchen or a service entrance. Because trophy houses require so much maintenance, service vehicles should also be able to drive all the way around the house. This doesn't mean that a loop needs paving, or even a layer of gravel or bark chips, although you may want to do that, at least during construction. During maintenance at the back of the house, it will be much more efficient if all the materials and equipment don't need to be carried around by hand. In many areas of the country, grass will work when the ground isn't too wet. Six or seven feet of width is sufficient for pick-up trucks.

It is also expected that larger homes will include space for vehicles to turn around so they won't need to back out into the street. Keep this in mind when planning for vehicle circulation.

THE COUNTRY HOUSE

Many of the principles for trophy houses also apply to the country house, regardless of size. It will still need ample parking for guests, since parking along rural roads isn't usually possible. If the property will have horses or other livestock, space is required for the maneuvering and parking of trailers as well.

Access will obviously be required for barns or other outbuildings, such as for a well house, even if only for occasional maintenance. As with the trophy house, in many climates these secondary accesses need not be paved, but they shouldn't be blocked with landscaping or other obstructions.

A common omission in the planning for a country house is the large cost of lengthy driveways (and of bringing utilities to the house the same distance). The fire department may require a minimum driveway width, as well as space to turn their trucks around. Be sure to get a cost estimate that includes a price per lineal foot, so that as various configurations are considered, the cost implications can be considered. Ensure the width of the driveway works for larger vehicles turning into the property.

Vehicles should be able to turn around and enter the rural road going forward. Visibility at the driveway entrance is crucial; watch for vertical and horizonal curves or vegetation that restrict views. Most rural roads were built when cars drove slower, and their sight lines are sometimes very limited. Joy riders (especially motorcycles) will exceed the speed limit substantially. It is a sad fact that the very features which make rural roads scenic also make them much more dangerous than suburban or urban streets.

If the sight distance is limited, consider moving the driveway, or removing some vegetation. If neither of those will solve the problem, perhaps the county road department will agree to lower the speed limit, or post some new signage regarding a curve.

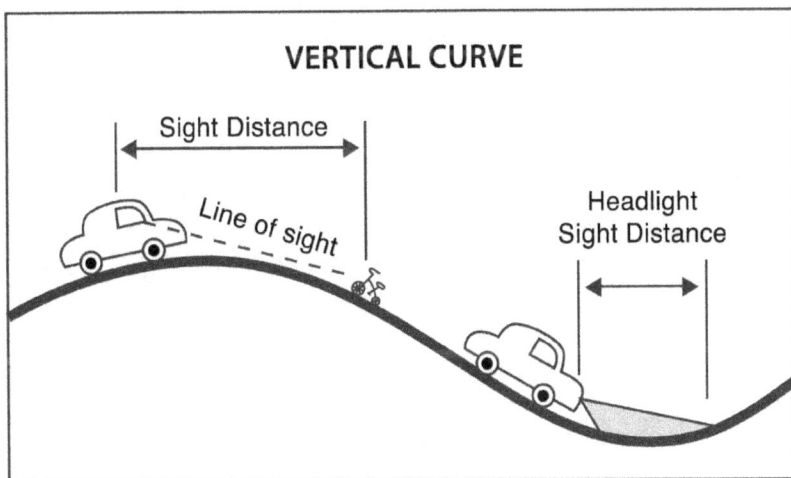

VERTICAL CURVE

Sight Distance

Line of sight

Headlight
Sight Distance

COLLECTOR STREETS IN A NEIGHBORHOOD

Local streets lead to the larger street and highway system. The streets that bring local traffic to arterials and highways are called collectors. Collector streets may or may not appear wider than local streets, but are expected to handle more traffic.

Depending on the time of day, a collector may not have much more traffic than a local street, but check at rush hour. In most communities some local streets are short-cuts and effectively serve as collectors. This is especially true in grid street systems. Eventually some of these streets are reclassified as collectors in belated recognition of their actual function. In other neighborhoods, local opposition may prevent the reclassification, and even may demand actions to reduce cut-through traffic. Many families (including my own) buy a house on a narrow residential street only to later be dismayed by an increase in the traffic. My mother wouldn't stand for the widening from two lanes to four, and we moved.

ARTERIAL STREETS IN A NEIGHBORHOOD

Arterial streets are the next step up from collector streets. They are typically at least four lanes wide (and more typically five). When arterial streets cross through residential areas, several things happen.

First, driveways onto arterials are discouraged and often prohibited. In more modern subdivisions, the back of the lots will face the arterial. While this solves the driveway problem, the back yards are noisier. Ideally, a sound wall, or at least a tall and sturdy fence and some hedges separate the arterial from the single family lots.

Where a narrower street is widened to become an arterial, driveways may still lead directly onto the arterial, which makes getting in and out of the driveway tougher. Front yards and driveways can become awkwardly short.

PRIVATE STREETS AND ACCESS RESTRICTIONS

Regardless of the street pattern, there are two circumstances where the street and access issues for single-family neighborhoods are governed by private arrangements. The first is developments with private streets. The second is developments with public streets where restrictions are located in

Covenants, Conditions, and Restrictions (CC&Rs, or CCRs) administered by a homeowners association.

In the first instance, many older subdivisions, gated communities, and unincorporated neighborhoods, the streets are privately owned by an association. Each lot has easement rights to use the street, and pays dues for maintenance. This arrangement will be revealed by a title search. Speak with the person responsible for collecting dues and managing the maintenance. This can be a hidden cost, so again, read and understand the title report – or get someone to help. It can be quite a surprise when you phone the local transportation agency to request plowing or repairs, and are abruptly informed that that maintaining the street is your responsibility. Some private streets are very well built, managed and maintained; others, not so well.

The second circumstance is when the streets are public, but access and parking issues are governed by CC&Rs. Many subdivisions restrict the width of driveways and/or the outdoor parking of boats and RVs. If you like these large things, be sure to check.

For both types, recognize that the legal width of the right-of-way usually exceeds the width of the pavement, so the landscaping along the pavement is probably not completely yours, although you are expected to maintain it. Find out where the boundary line is.

SIGHT TRIANGLE
(Vision Clearance Triangle)

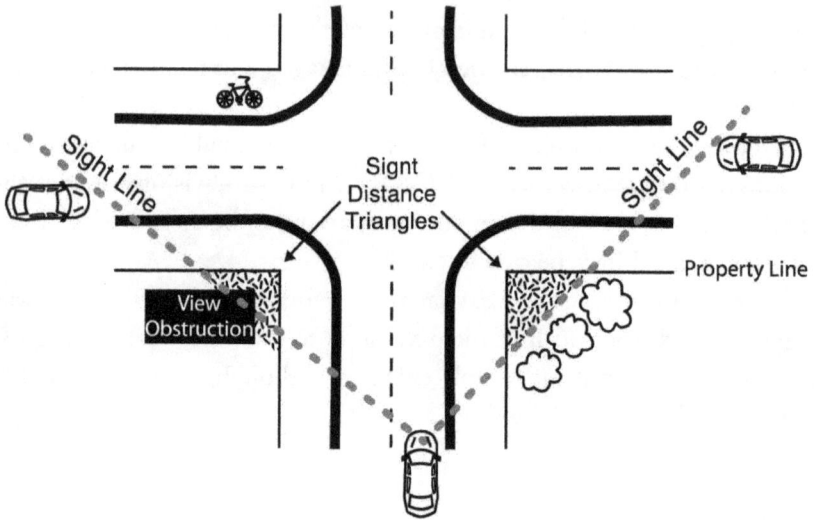

Sight Line

Sight Line

Sight Line

Signt Distance Triangles

View Obstruction

Property Line

Chapter Ten

SUBURBAN MULTI FAMILY

Suburban multi family developments take many forms, and most are two or three stories. This chapter is written with the garden apartment format in mind, ranging from a few dozen units up to several hundred.

The big access issue for garden apartments is the position of the main entrance as viewed from the busiest adjacent street. The location of the access will be driven by the classification of that street and whether it allows access, or whether access must be taken from a side street. We have all driven by apartment building after apartment building set back behind an attractive landscape buffer and wondered where the driveway is. If passersby only see the backs of the units, with their assortment of bikes and barbecues, that is something less than welcoming, and a privacy concern for tenants.

Ideally, the main entrance is spacious, inviting, and on the busiest street, so passersby can see the entry signage and look directly into the property. For many larger complexes, amenities such as pools and community recreation buildings are placed just behind the entry for visibility from the street. If access must be taken from a side street, use extra signage to direct the traffic. The closer the access is to the intersection with the primary street, the better.

There are two schools of thought regarding the number of access driveways. One school prefers just a single driveway, which is easier to monitor for security, and eliminates cut-through traffic. The peak turning movement will be left turns out during the morning rush hour. Be sure it flows well. Wayfinding is especially important for single entrance developments, so place a good map of the layout near the driveway access.

The other school likes multiple driveways because it minimizes the amount of drive aisles that must be built and maintained within the property. This frees up space for additional landscaping or more apartments. In addition, traffic is not concentrated at one main entrance, which is an inconvenience for nearby apartments. Some properties have public streets running through them. The public streets are maintained by the transportation agency and the extra traffic integrates the complex with the surrounding neighborhood. This prevents the confining, crowded feeling that enclosed complexes experience.

I have an affection for a great city. I feel safe in the neighborhood of man, and enjoy the sweet security of the streets.

Henry Wadsworth Longfellow

CHAPTER ELEVEN
URBAN MULTIFAMILY

As areas become more urban and dense, the dominance of the automobile gradually recedes, and more people will access properties by other means. Of course, vehicle access is still important, but it becomes more difficult to compete with other demands and place a driveway effectively on the site. Urban multifamily locations fall into three basic categories: sites without driveways or alleys, and sites with only alleys, sites with conventional driveways.

For sites without driveways or alleys, there obviously will not be any parking or loading on the site itself. Given that everything must be brought on to the property by hand, how can service vehicles park as close as possible? Vehicles that need access include delivery vehicles trying to access the front entry or a service sidewalk, and service vehicles that will desire access to all parts of the building for maintenance.

Deliveries to the front of the building are best served by an on-street loading space. This may need to be negotiated with the local transportation agency, and may be opposed by people who prefer that service vehicles park elsewhere. Many cities place loading spaces at the end of a block where larger vehicles can use the area of an intersection for maneuvering in and out of the loading space. Some cities are amenable to very short term parking spaces on the street directly in front of a building to allow for passengers to be picked up and dropped off, and service vehicles will also use these spaces.

When better access is needed, for example, when the roof is being replaced, arrangements must be made with the local transportation agency to temporarily close on-street parking in order to provide spaces for equipment and vehicles. This will take some time, so plan ahead and be prepared for some complaints, especially if the contractor isn't actively working while the spaces are blocked. For less time-consuming access, such as for the weekly waste hauler pickup, don't expect any special accommodations from the city; these vehicles may need to stop in the traffic lane.

If the multifamily site is served by an alley, chances are there will not be much, if any, vehicle access in the front. Service vehicles and loading should use the alley whenever possible. If the alley is narrow, such as in downtown Seattle, parking is not allowed when a vehicle is not being actively loaded or unloaded. Where enough width is available, service vehicles can park, and there isn't much of a problem.

Alleys are a good place for access to parking garages as well because the front of the building can be more visually attractive. Urban alleys naturally present security challenges, so look for good lighting and good camera angles at the entrance. If they are not available, rearrange them or there will be difficulty in renting units.

Urban multifamily sites with conventional driveways are rare, and typically occur when an older mansion was converted into apartments or condominiums. In this circumstance, the challenge tends to be more with the parking than with the driveway access. Most often the driveway will face a garage door. Check whether the driveway is long enough for service vehicles to park without blocking the sidewalk.

When urban multifamily buildings include retail storefronts, access for loading, of course, becomes more important. With storefront office uses, not so much. The building will have separate entrances for the residential and commercial areas, but separate loading areas are rare. Commercial loading usually occurs during business hours (except in the largest downtowns, when they occur at night), while residential tenants will use loading spaces at all hours, so a shared loading space can work in that sense. Locating the loading space conveniently for both uses is the challenging task.

On the regulatory side, the key issue is whether a curb cut is allowed, and if so, where and how wide. The city may be more concerned about pedestrians using the sidewalk than vehicles trying to access your building. Think carefully about your access needs, and then see what the city is willing to accommodate.

The key internal access issue for mixed use urban multifamily developments is what tenants have what rights to what access and loading facilities.

For existing buildings, this should be spelled out in the leases, and for commercial leases it often is. Residential leases often aren't so thorough. In the absence of clear lease terms, it's frustrating and time consuming to referee disputes among the tenants. Problems also occur when the rights are carefully described in the leases, but are ignored or do not serve the tenants well. Tenants are exasperated by rules which get in their way, especially when they see a loading area that is infrequently used.

Americans will put up with anything
provided it doesn't block traffic.

Dan Rather

Chapter Twelve

ROWHOUSES

For rowhouses, the vehicle entrance (if there is one) can be in front or back. For units at the end of the row, a side entrance may be possible as well, but this requires units that are more than 20 feet wide, for a car to park perpendicular to the main axis of the unit.

ACCESS IN THE FRONT

Since rowhouses tend to be narrow, the primary challenge of placing vehicle entrances in the front is to keep the driveway and garage entrance from overwhelming the rest of the façade. This challenge is best addressed by limiting the garage door to a single car width. Then the garage itself can be deep enough to accommodate two cars (a tandem garage). Of course, this means that one car will block the other, but sometimes that cannot be prevented.

Try to place the garage door at least 18 or 20 feet behind the back of the sidewalk so a car can park in front of the garage without blocking the sidewalk. If the garage door cannot be set back that far, most architects place it right at the sidewalk. San Francisco's Marina District has many examples of garage doors just behind the sidewalk. Many cities have regulations that address this situation.

A variety of design tools can be used to reduce the visual impact of multiple driveways and garage doors in the front. For example, cantilevering the second level a couple feet beyond the garage door will cast shadows over the door and draw the eye to the façade of the level above. Lowering the grade of the garage entrance so that cars must drive down into it can also accomplish this. A less complicated method is to place an arbor or trellis over the top of the garage, which draws attention to the plants and again casts shadows over the garage door.

ACCESS IN THE BACK

This method enhances the front of the building by allowing for more landscaping and pedestrian amenities. Doing so requires alleys, whether public or private. The deeper the lots, the easier it will be to fit the alley, garage, and/or surface parking.

On a sloped lot, the alley and garages can be on a lower or higher level than the front entrance. If the alley is on a higher level, a split level design works better than having the alley and garage up at the second level because it reduces the number of stairs and allows natural light into the back of the units.

When the garage and alley are a full level below, the garages become like daylight basements, which saves square footage for living space above and allows natural light into all levels of living space at the back of the units. The down side is the need for internal stairs to reach the living space. However, since rowhouses are already vertically oriented, the target market is not as sensitive to stairs as the general population.

Another advantage of placing the vehicle entrance in the back is that the vehicle entrance doesn't need to compete with the pedestrian entrance for frontage width, and thus can often be wide enough for a double garage door.

This pattern is found in Baltimore in the area between Federal Hill and Riverside Park.

ACCESS FOR EMERGENCY AND SERVICE VEHICLES

Regardless of the driveway location, rowhouses should provide access from the back for service and emergency vehicles. If alleys will be used, check with the local fire department and waste hauler to ensure their trucks can navigate them. If not, be ready to install a turnaround for their trucks. Without such a turnaround, the fire department will likely insist on sprinklers or extra hydrants to compensate.

Regarding other service vehicles, someday the back of the units will need to be repainted and reroofed. Even if there isn't an alley, try to include some sort of paved path wide enough for a full size pickup; eight feet at a minimum. Ideally, the path will be level enough for a man lift to operate safely. The more challenging the access for service vehicles, the more difficult (read expensive) the maintenance will be, because service crews unable to drive their equipment into place will use more labor.

Societies need rules that make no sense for individuals. For example, it makes no difference whether a single car drives on the left or on the right. But it makes all the difference when there are many cars.

Marvin Minsky

CHAPTER THIRTEEN

RETAIL MAIN STREET

In prosperous areas, traditional main streets are making a comeback; however, their vehicle access and parking cannot readily be altered. On-street parking is either parallel or angled. While parallel parking can accommodate oversize spaces reserved for trucks and loading, angled parking requires more street width and can accommodate more cars.

Parking and loading rules will be driven by the street classification. The local transportation agency should have a person who manages on-street parking and loading. Expect controversy when the number and placement of loading spaces is being discussed. Some merchants will insist on car parking only because when a loading space is occupied by a truck or van, storefront visibility is blocked. Sometimes curbside loading areas are restricted by bulky street trees. Most shopkeepers prefer to have the trees, but if they are the wrong species or are not pruned, they may make it difficult for taller service vehicles to park.

Many traditional main streets have alley access in back. These are often gritty and narrow but sufficient for deliveries and service vehicles, and in older urban areas they may also provide access for retail shoppers. Of special importance is whether any neighbors abuse the alley privileges, causing blockages (read delays) or messes (think boxes at best). A poorly managed alley is a chronic headache.

Determine how well the city actively handles amenities such as lighting, drainage, and snow removal. If the alley is not well maintained, and the city is unresponsive, are the neighbors willing to pitch in? The simplest things for property owners to improve are lighting and cleanliness, so start there.

Retail shoppers expect convenient parking, and most of the access described in this book leads straight to parking. In upscale suburban areas, structured parking may be an option. But if not, ask hard questions about where customers, employees, and residents (if there are apartments on top) park. Almost as important is the experience of walking from the parking area to the main street. Is it a pleasant walk from a leafy residential side street, or an awkward walk past an unsightly industrial property, or something in between? In some cities, downtown property owners pay extra taxes to support a parking garage. Lifestyle center developments provide sufficient remote parking within walking distance of the faux main street. In other words, vehicle access for a main street property may really mean vehicle access to the closest available parking lot or garage.

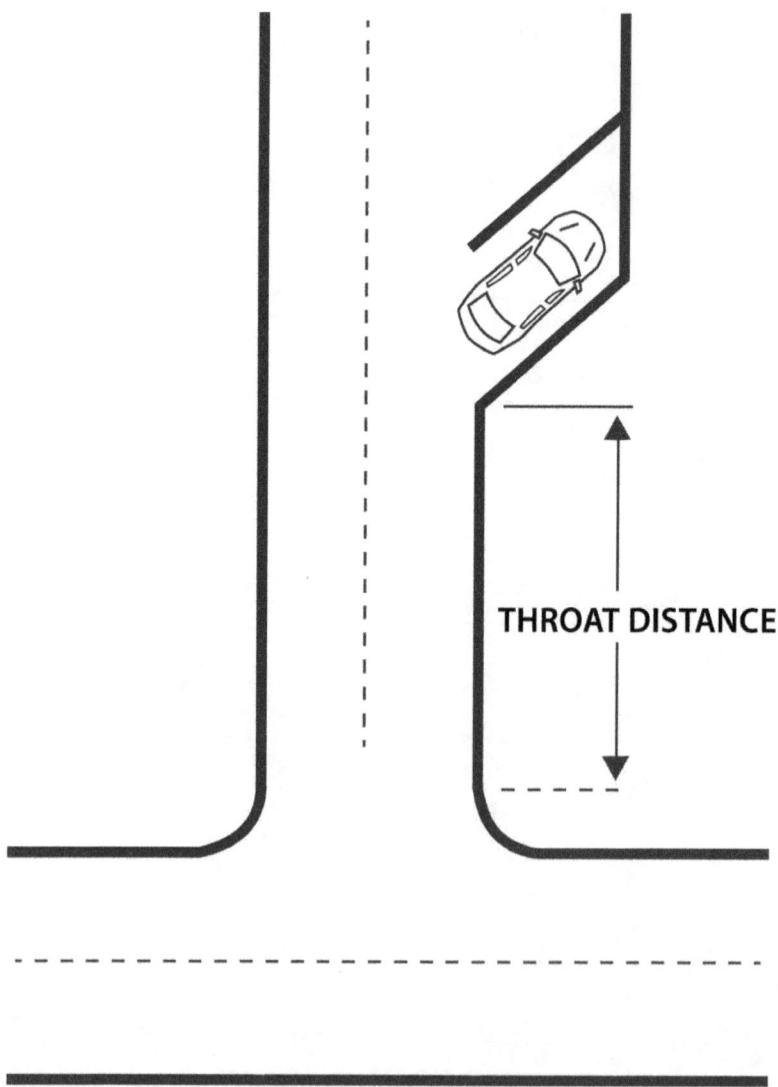

THROAT DISTANCE

CHAPTER FOURTEEN

THE RETAIL COMMERCIAL STRIP

The retail strip comes in a variety of formats, which are driven by the depth of the property, meaning the distance from the street to the back property line. The depth of strips ranges from a minimum of about 100 feet to a maximum of about 1000 feet. Of course, the street frontage lengths vary as well, but generally speaking, the length of a block exceeds the depth of the lots, which gives strips their linear character. The access issues for strips vary based on the depth, so this chapter includes three sections for shallow, medium and deep commercial strips.

Strips of all sizes share some common features. Individual properties are often evaluated for the length of their frontage, which translates into visibility for vehicles driving by, and time for the vehicles to slow down and enter an access. Visibility is also inversely proportional to the traffic speed - the faster the traffic, the less time there is for a person riding in a vehicle to see the driveway and slow down to enter.

The ratio of the frontage to the depth determines the shape of the property, which in turn determines options for the site plan. The higher the ratio, the more parallel the property is to the strip. A ratio of one to one is a square. Ratios less than one are unusual on commercial strips and should be approached with caution. These narrow properties only function well when the frontage is wide enough for visibility and there is secondary access located toward the back of the property. Examples of secondary access are access from the side, as on a corner lot, or a lot with reciprocal easements with abutting properties. Secondary access can occur from the rear, from an alley or street that is parallel to the strip. Without a secondary access toward the rear, an unusually large portion of the property is consumed by a driveway extending to the back, which is used infrequently, mostly for loading. The width of that area takes away from the lineal feet of storefront. It is often hard to see, and thus, a security problem. For these properties, see if the driveway can accommodate more uses, such as waste storage or employee parking. Sometimes these driveways are required for fire department access. If so, determine whether other fire safety features such as upgraded walls, sprinklers, or an extra hydrant can substitute for a fire lane.

At many successful strips, very little square footage within the property is consumed by a driveway for vehicle access to the rear, often because the rear of the property is accessed from a public right-of-way.

Many shallow and medium-depth strips were not designed to accommodate larger or even medium-size trucks, which can be both a benefit and a detriment. On the positive side, valuable real estate is not taken up for truck maneuvering and a loading space that is used infrequently. The catch is that in the absence of a dedicated loading area, delivery trucks block the regular traffic pattern somewhere, perhaps in the parking lot, the drive aisle, or on the street. None of these options encourage customers to enter the property, and some will irritate neighbors, vendors, the waste hauler, service crews, passersby, and the transportation agency.

Commercial strips are located on busy streets, usually arterials. Access is largely determined by the historic evolution of the properties making up the strip. Traditionally, each property had its own driveway. As traffic increases, multiple driveways become problematic, since vehicles getting on and off the street at so many locations impede traffic flow. Traffic flows faster and more safely when there are fewer driveways, so in most congested areas, transportation agencies endeavor to reduce the number of driveways, and increase the distance between driveways whenever possible.

Regardless of the number of access points or their particular type, the key elements of an entrance driveway are the visibility and ease of use, combined with the visibility of the property and signage. The ideal situation is a traffic signal along with dedicated lanes for turning right and left into the property. To qualify for a traffic signal (i.e., meeting a signal warrant) usually requires at least 8 acres of retail property. Strips less than 600 feet deep are unlikely to have enough traffic to justify a traffic signal. The advantages of a signalized entrance are that left turns can be made comfortably and safely, and everyone stopped during a red light is able to view the property.

Consolidating the access at one location in a strip development creates winners and losers among the stores within the strip, as those located closer to the main access are the most visible. When there are multiple owners within the strip, this issue is especially contentious, and trade-offs will occur. For example, a retail property may be better off with its own driveway on a two- or three-lane street, or it may be better to close the driveway, but have more traffic flowing by on a four- or five-lane street. There is a sweet spot that will vary depending on the local circumstances. If vehicles can see the storefronts well from the street, and see where to turn into the property to get to the store, you are better off with fewer driveways and more windshields passing by the property each day. The situation to avoid is when either the store or the access is hard to see from a passing vehicle.

A related issue is left turn access. When traffic isn't congested, left turns into strip property are typically allowed. As traffic gets heavier, the preference is to eliminate left turns. Retailers complain that elimination of left turns effectively makes the street one way, and there is some truth in that perspective. The access issue is whether there is a convenient alternative access that does not require a left turn into the driveway on the primary street. Perhaps a U-turn is possible at the next signal. Is a left turn permitted at the next signal allowing cars to enter the property from a side street?

A second issue for strips without left turn access is the direction of commute traffic. Property on the side of the street that is busy in the morning may work for a pancake house, but most retail uses are busier during the late afternoon and will fare poorly. Property on the side that is busy during the afternoon commute is better, which is not to say that it is good.

What matters is the number of vehicles passing the property with a straightforward opportunity to enter the driveway, which may well be a smaller number than you think. If you ask the local transportation agency for the traffic counts on a commercial street, they will typically tell you the total number of vehicles going both directions on an average day. For our purposes, only vehicles which have a relatively simple route into the driveway should be counted.

If a substantial portion of the half that does have a simple route into the driveway is zipping by on the way to work in the morning, you need to discount those vehicles accordingly. If in doubt – and you should always be in doubt – hire a traffic counter to check. Counts are economical, and you can obtain them without engaging the services of a traffic engineer. At a minimum, get out there during the morning and afternoon commutes to see the flow of traffic and the operation of area driveways for yourself.

With that background, let's move on to the three types of commercial strip properties: the shallow strips less than 200 feet deep, medium strips between 200 and 500 feet deep, and the deep strips more than 500 feet deep.

THE SHALLOW STRIP

Strips up to 200 feet deep are typically limited to a single row of storefronts facing the street, with buildings placed close to the back property line so there is no vehicle access around the side of the building. Perhaps there is an alley. For existing strips you can, of course, walk around back there, and make a decision about whatever you find.

For new development, the local government will have rules about how close the building can be to the back property line. There will be zoning rules about side setbacks, perimeter landscaping, and loading, and the fire department may require a clear path for their trucks. Be sure to understand these rules before starting work on a site plan.

The shallow strip will typically have a parking aisle, either single or double loaded, parallel to the street. The access driveway tends to have a very short throat. The trouble with short throats is they lack capacity for more than one or two vehicles. If someone is backing out of a parking space, and someone else is waiting to get into that space, and a third vehicle wants to enter the driveway, the third vehicle may not be able to turn off the street. This is a recipe for rear-end collisions. One thing to check is the speed limit of the street. The higher the speed limit, the higher the risk of rear-end collisions.

Again, watch what happens at the driveway during the busiest part of the day to see if this is a problem, and keep the occupancy in mind when doing so. If you are analyzing a property with some vacancy, congestion may only become apparent after the property is fully occupied.

In commercial strips, the fire department is concerned about getting trucks as close as possible to the flames, and is also concerned about fire spreading from one store to another. Their strong preference will be for a driveway around the back of the building. For shallow strip properties where that isn't possible, expect to pay for alternative fire suppression.

Most older, shallow strips lack a dedicated loading area, so review the operational consequences. First, look at the waste storage, and see whether there is a way to screen it that works for the hauler. The second issue is vendor deliveries, which is more complicated, since the sizes of delivery trucks vary greatly. Most shallow strips will not include one of the larger franchises or stores serviced by full-size trucks. It is important know what the mix of delivery vehicles is, and what it may become with different tenants.

Learn where the trucks stop to unload and how that interrupts the traffic flow. If the trucks stop in a drive aisle, check the width of the aisle. The standard width is 24 feet for double-loaded 90-degree parking, but a few extra feet go a long way toward making truck turns possible. If things are too tight, see if a parking space at the end of a row can be sacrificed to make more room for the entry or exit of trucks.

Look for lease provisions that specify when and where loading can occur and see if those provisions are being followed. Also, ask whether it is practical to enforce whatever lease provisions there may be. Sometimes there just is not a simple solution.

On shallow strips, ideally there will be one driveway at each side of the property, plus at least one driveway onto the primary street. That way, the internal traffic flow can move in a forward direction without having to turn around. This is both more convenient for customers and saves space. If only one driveway is available, hopefully it will be in the center of the property, and turning space for vehicles – including larger delivery vehicles – will be required.

For a good example of a vintage shallow strip, look along the north side of West Lovers Lane in Dallas, Texas which extends east from the Love Field airport.

THE MEDIUM DEPTH COMMERCIAL STRIP

Strips between 200 and 500 feet deep differ from the shallow strip in ways that affect access. A medium depth strip property should have convenient access to a dedicated loading area. If not, chances are it is an older center that could stand some updating, so think about where one might be put in. And, don't be surprised if the local government compels you to get it done. Bear in mind that larger trucks can be expected in these larger centers, so check the maneuvering room around the loading area. These properties should have a secondary access located on the side from a public street or an abutting property, or in the rear from an alley or another street.

The secondary access should lead directly to the loading area or directly to the customer parking area.

The primary driveway entrance should be wide enough for three lanes - typically one for entering, one for exiting with a left turn, and the third for exiting with a right turn. Throats should be longer to account for the higher number of cars that need to use the driveway. Be careful about drive aisles intersecting with the throat, as this kind of intersection can cause congestion at the entrance.

A successful medium depth strip is found on U.S. Highway 67 in the northeast section of Little Rock, Arkansas.

THE DEEP COMMERCIAL STRIP

Strips deeper than 500 feet should have excellent access features, starting with a loading area that is served by a dedicated access that serves no other purpose, except perhaps employee parking. That access should come from a public street to the side or the rear of the property. The largest trucks are routine in these larger centers, so check the maneuvering room around the loading area. In addition to the loading spaces for the largest trucks, make sure there is space for smaller service vehicles to park and unload as well.

Second, full depth properties should have a secondary access just for customers, whether located on the side from a public street or an abutting property. The secondary access should lead directly to the customer parking area. Right turn only access works well in this context, so long as a sufficient deceleration lane is provided.

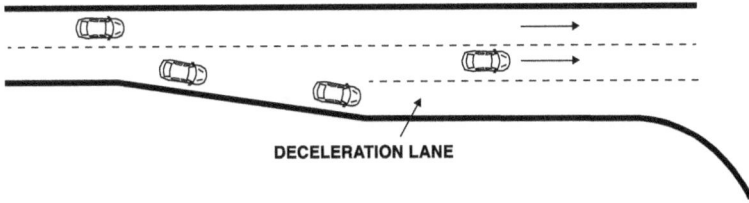

DECELERATION LANE

Third, the width of the primary driveway entrance must be wide enough for three or more lanes, depending on the capacity and location of the secondary access driveways, and should be signalized.

Deep strips should have signalized access. If there is a signalized entrance, you may not need a second access point on the main street. Without a signal or a second access onto the main street, be sure there is at least one access leading onto a side street that intersects with the main street, preferably at a signalized intersection.

The nature of the tenant spaces is also important. The fewer the tenants and the larger the stores, the easier it is to manage with fewer access points. It also allows for simpler signage and perhaps a signalized entrance. Multiple access points without a clearly visible main entrance can be confusing.

With more tenants and smaller stores, it is sometimes better to have multiple access points located close to the different areas of the strip center. If you use a main, potentially signalized, access in this type of strip center, then some stores will be much more visible than others.

Deeper strip properties often have building pads in front along the primary street, which take access from a side street or an internal aisle. When these pads include drive through restaurants, special attention must be given to the depth of the throat to ensure adequate storage capacity during the afternoon rush hour. Many older deep strip properties were developed without pad restaurants in mind. Without sufficient storage in the throat, the internal circulation of the property may become congested and frustrating for customers. Check the plans for complete build out of the property – just because the access and throat operate smoothly today does not mean they can accommodate more pads. Sit-down restaurants and banks do not generate as much traffic as a drive-through restaurant, so check if the uses on future pads are controlled, and if so, by whom.

Drive-in banks were established so most of the cars today could see their real owners.

E. Joseph Cossman

CHAPTER FIFTEEN
DRIVE-THROUGH RETAIL

Drive-through businesses are designed for a consistent stream of vehicles to enter and exit the property without parking, while other vehicles park. While this book is not about internal vehicle circulation but for drive-through uses, the unusually close relationship of the access points to the internal circulation merits some discussion.

To operate well, the access points must lead directly to both the parking area and to the drive-through lane, and the drive-through lane must have enough storage capacity to separate waiting vehicles from the parking area and doors. The drive-through lane usually forms a loop around the building, and the access points should be placed at the beginning and the end of the loop. The exit lane, or throat, must be long enough to store vehicles waiting to get on to the street without backing up the drive-through window.

Most drive-through businesses have at least two access points. If only one access point is possible, an unusually large portion of the site must be devoted to circulation. This increases the risk that the circulation will interfere with the parking area or pedestrian paths. On a larger property, these risks can be overcome, but on smaller properties conflicts must be expected.

Service and delivery vehicles take advantage of the proportionally large amount of internal circulation space on most drive-through properties. But, of course, you still need to ensure these vehicle stay clear of the customer traffic. As always, check with the trash hauler before you buy or build. If you are pitching a site to a potential franchise, they will likely have their own design people to work out these details.

For drive-through properties, the drive-through itself presents a wayfinding issue. Drivers entering the property should clearly see the drive-through lane and a separate route to parking. If not, then drivers will pause upon entering with the consequent risks of traffic delays and rear end collisions. At a minimum, drivers should be directed to the drive-through with good signage and striping. Landscaping can also be used to distinguish the drive-through lane from the rest of the circulation and parking. The risk of poor visibility is increased on sites where the drive-through window and the ordering station are toward the back of the property. While that may be an advantage for circulation reasons, ask how someone driving by at street speed will realize that drive-through service is available.

Drive-through sites fall into three basic categories – corner, mid-block, and shopping center pads.

CORNER

For corner properties, ideally there would be one access on each street, which allows one access point to primarily serve the parking and one access point to primarily serve the drive-through.

Be aware that innumerable restaurants built in this pattern have been severely harmed by increases in street traffic that were either unanticipated or misunderstood. Normally, traffic increases are a good thing. However, if the traffic on the street leading toward the intersection (the upstream traffic) increases to the tipping point where vehicles stopped behind a red light block the driveway, then customers can't get in or out, especially during the dinner rush. On either street, if traffic increases to the point where vehicles cannot turn left in or left out of the driveway, more customers will be lost.

Likewise, if traffic increases to the point where the transportation agency decides to add lanes to the intersection, the new lanes may take a slice off the edge of the property. It is crucial to know whether the internal circulation will be able to continue in its current layout. Frequently it won't. As a precautionary measure, you may be able to build further back to leave room for a future widening, but that does not mean the access points will operate smoothly.

There is a huge difference between a good corner site in a mature area with enough traffic to support the drive-through use and a good corner site in a growing area where the access points have a limited life expectancy.

MID-BLOCK

For mid-block locations, ideally there will be one access point at each of the front corners of the property. This allows the loop to be in the shape of a U, with the front of the building up against the sidewalk for maximum visibility. The tricky part here is to ensure that vehicles turning left into the property are dissuaded from trying to pull into the drive-through exit. Solutions include good signage and a pork chop. If there is only one access point, a loop will need to go completely around the building and thus will consume more real estate.

PADS

Pads are insulated from many of the access problems experienced by stand-alone sites. Pads utilize reverse loading, that is, the access points are located behind the building as seen from the street. Vehicles enter the shopping center and use its internal circulation to reach the drive-through business. The access points to the pad site itself are usually straightforward. In this setting, adequate capacity at the shopping center access and its throat is the thing to watch for, especially during the afternoon rush hour.

When shopping was still connected to the street it was also an intensification and articulation of the street. Now it has become utterly independent, contained, controlled, surveyed.

Rem Koolhas

Chapter Sixteen

THE GROCERY-ANCHORED NEIGHBORHOOD CENTER

The modern grocery-anchored center is a retail project of 10-20 acres with 100,000 square feet, or more, of retail space that serves a local market area with groceries plus a variety of smaller retail uses. The one nearest my home includes a hardware store, an ice cream shop, Mexican and Chinese sit down restaurants, a craft shop, a drug store, an optometrist, a beauty and tanning salon, and a teen drop-in center. The concept is that everyone shops for groceries regularly, and since they are coming for food, let's include a few other things they might want to have at the same time.

THE ENTRANCE

These properties work best with a signalized main entrance. Secondary entrances, including a loading entrance, are often placed on side streets. While multiple entrances may seem ideal, and certainly ease the flow of traffic into and out of the center, the lack of a main entrance can detract from the identity of the center. If the signage and entrances are spread around the property, it feels like several properties rather than a unified center. Of course, the whole idea of a unified center is to encourage shoppers to visit multiple stores during their visit.

Returning to the central issue of access and traffic, for retail it is more important to have a convenient entrance than a convenient exit. Where a left turn directly into the center is impossible, first see if you can install a signal. If not, make the right-in entry as prominent and welcoming as you can. Slip lanes are ideal for this purpose. Yes, they consume extra real estate, but today's distracted drivers will appreciate the ease of a dedicated lane for slowing down before the turn. There is a school of thought that while slip lanes are beneficial to vehicles entering the property, they also allow other vehicles to more easily drive past it instead of slowing down behind the vehicles turning right into the property. The thinking is that while they slow down, they view the property and the signage and may decide in the moment, or in the future, to visit. The corollary is that slip lanes allow vehicles to slow down and make the turn without worrying about getting rear-ended.

SIGNALS

A signalized entrance is preferred because it allows more vehicles to more easily enter (and exit) the property. Qualifying for a signal requires a signal warrant, which is traffic speak for a sufficient number of vehicles to justify ("warrant") the trouble and expense of installing and maintaining a signal.

For the grocery-anchored center, a three lane entrance is standard - one entering, one exiting to the right, plus an exit lane for going straight and left turns combined. Depending on local conditions, sometimes there is a dedicated left turn lane, and a shared lane for going straight and right turns. Of course, there are variations on this, but three lanes is the basic design.

Naturally, the front façade of the grocery anchor and its parking lot must be visible from the entrance, but the other stores should also be clearly visible to entering vehicles. At the same time, the street entrance itself must present a clear way forward, lest shoppers enter the center only to be perplexed by the layout and unsure of where to go next.

This problem occurs even in well-designed centers, so the engineering question is how long the throat needs to be for entering vehicles. That is, how far into the center should a vehicle travel before being confronted with a decision about which way to proceed? Another key question is the amount and location of loading spaces. The answers to these questions largely depend on the basic layout of the center, which is usually determined by its relationship to the adjacent streets.

RELATION TO STREET PATTERNS

We'll look at three street frontage patterns, and describe their implications for placement and design of the access and truck loading: frontage on a single street, frontage at a corner, and frontage on three sides.

SINGLE FRONTAGE

When the center has frontage on a single street, there will be abutting commercial property on both sides, which tends to limit visibility into the center. Naturally, this is why a longer frontage is always better, since the property owner has control over the number and placement of visual obstructions, at least outside the right-of-way. Traditionally, the grocery anchor was placed behind the parking lot; however, because of the visibility constraints, some prefer (and some jurisdictions now mandate) to place the grocery store right along the frontage, with the smaller stores behind the parking field.

When the center fronts on a single street, it is difficult to separate the truck traffic from the customer entrance. Inevitably, this consumes a substantial amount of real estate, which is one reason why locations on a corner are preferred. The traditional layout is for a single main entrance flanked by a large sign. When the entrance serves trucks, it must be substantially wider than an entrance that just serves cars. If the throat driveway is narrow, the curb radius at the entrance must be correspondingly larger to allow truck turns. In other words, the wider the driveway is where it meets the street, the narrower the throat can be, and vice versa.

The throat should afford a direct and unobstructed view to the main entrance of the grocery store. The smaller stores can be placed in a line next to the grocery store, or perpendicular to it, so long as the drive aisle in front of the stores leads directly to the throat and street access.

CORNER LOCATIONS

For centers on a corner, the main entrance will preferably be placed on the main street, although government access restrictions may require the access to be on the side street. We'll look at each type. When the main entrance is on the main street, it can be designed for cars without worrying about large trucks. The side street entrance is preferably placed in line with the front of the anchor store. The side street entrance then leads directly to the busy drive aisle that runs along the store frontage. Then, a second side street entrance is placed behind the stores for truck access to the loading area. Sometimes employee parking is also provided behind the store.

The essential advantage is that the side street provides easy access to both the drive aisle along the storefronts and for the loading area in the rear. Because that access occurs on the public street, the property benefits from additional visibility, and it saves a substantial amount of real estate since less circulation space is needed within the property.

FULL BLOCK WIDTH – STREETS ON THREE SIDES

When the center has streets on three sides, the drive aisle along the storefront can connect to accesses at both streets, and a parallel aisle for loading in the rear can do the same. Again, the key consideration is whether the main entrance will be on the main street or a side street. If on the main street, the entrance should create a view corridor to the grocery store.

If the entrance cannot be on the main street, first make sure that one, or preferably both, side streets meet the main street at a signalized intersection. Because vehicles on the main street will have a hard time seeing the driveway entrance, visibility of the stores is that much more important.

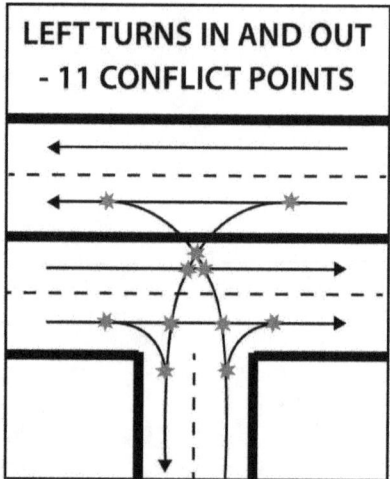

LEFT TURNS IN AND OUT
- 11 CONFLICT POINTS

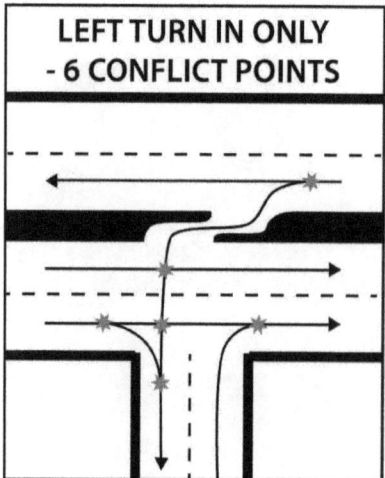

LEFT TURN IN ONLY
- 6 CONFLICT POINTS

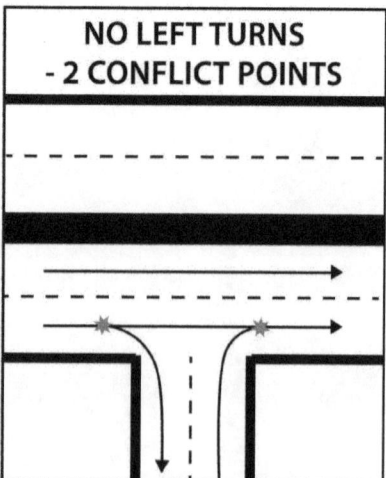

NO LEFT TURNS
- 2 CONFLICT POINTS

CHAPTER SEVENTEEN
THE LOW DENSITY OFFICE DEVELOPMENT

In suburban locations, single-story office parks are located where the cost of the land is low enough that multi-story development isn't necessary or feasible. Congestion at access points is less of a risk, and this drives the design of access. Low-density office parks usually will not warrant a signalized entrance, and more flexibility is possible for placement of the access, especially if taken from a local street. Presuming that flexibility, the question becomes whether to have many access points, or not. The tenants will appreciate direct access and good visibility, which translates to simple wayfinding. The wayfinding becomes more difficult if, after entering the property, drivers are faced with a maze. The more driveways, the closer each driveway will be to tenant spaces, and the easier it will be for visitors to find those spaces.

The trade-off is that each access point consumes real estate, and multiple access points can be confusing. Along curved streets, visibility depends on the sharpness of the curves and landscaping, so this rule is less applicable. The key thing is to distinguish each entrance with different landmarks. When the street pattern is a grid, and there are entrances on multiple frontages, the landmark can simply be the name of the street. When there are multiple entrances on a curved street, something must distinguish them, such as signage.

A good way to save real estate is to place several access points and parking areas around the perimeter of the property. Without drive aisles or parking in the middle, the amount of paving is minimized, which saves costs. This works for office properties because visitors usually visit only one tenant at a time. This is quite the opposite from some retail projects where access and internal circulation promote visibility of as many storefronts as possible.

When there is frontage on more than one street, there should be a driveway on each frontage. However, this should be coordinated with the signage, because you may only be allowed one major sign. In that case, you may end up with a primary access and sign on one frontage, and a secondary access and signage on the other frontage(s).

Emergency vehicles will expect good access to all sides of the buildings; however, this does not mean that the access must consume square footage within the property. If at least part of the building is placed close to a public street, the street can serve emergency vehicles, as least for that portion of the building. If the design preference is to have all buildings set well back from the street, then emergency vehicle access must be accommodated within the property.

Vehicles providing goods and services to low density office properties are typically small and do not often include full size trucks. The exception occurs when an office park also includes flex space occupied by light industrial tenants, in which case accommodations must be made for larger trucks.

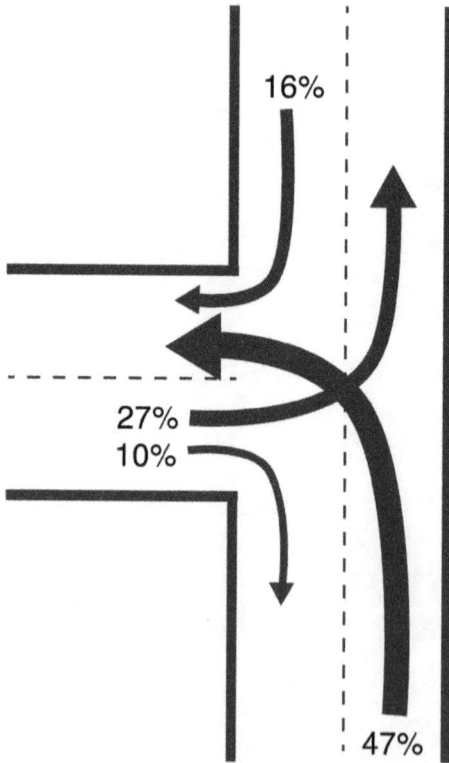

PERCENT OF CRASHES BY DRIVEWAY MOVEMENT

16%

27%
10%

47%

CHAPTER EIGHTEEN

SUBURBAN CORPORATE CAMPUS

THE ENTRANCE AND WAYFINDING

Corporate campuses prefer to have a minimum number of entrances for security reasons. Spread over many acres, the substantial internal circulation layout usually funnels into one or two access points.

Signals are strongly preferred at the primary entrance because the signal timing can be adapted to the alternating rush hour flow into and out of the campus. A secondary entrance may then be utilized for specialty use, such as a formal entry for visitors, or a truck entrance for loading.

Corporate campuses are less concerned about visibility than almost all other land uses. They discourage casual visitors, and often are shrouded by landscaping.

Suburban locations with surplus area for expansion are frequently selected. During initial development phases, the surplus area is landscaped. Where you see the broad lawns, others see future buildings and parking lots. For our purposes, think through how future expansions would utilize the current access, and whether additional access may be practical. As with regional shopping centers, corporate campuses place the parking at the edge, with the central areas reserved for buildings and pedestrian areas.

An exception to this rule is the former Union Carbide campus, nestled in the woods of Connecticut. Like the Dallas-Fort Worth airport, the campus is linear, with the main street forming the spine. The street leads straight into, and also through, a parking structure. Wings of the building span out from the parking garage. This design maximizes the views of the woods, in contrast to many office buildings that overlook parking.

Less is more.

Ludwig Mies van der Rohe

CHAPTER NINETEEN
URBAN OFFICE TOWER

The urban office tower requires access for passenger cars and service vehicles; however, unlike lower density development where these functions can be more easily separated, in the urban setting both functions usually need to be accommodated within one compact access location.

Parking access for cars is simple enough; the tough part is access for service vehicles, especially larger ones such as moving trucks.

The access should be perpendicular to the street. When it is not, valuable real estate is consumed for driveways which generally could be put to a more profitable use, such as retail storefronts. Sometimes just a little area is sacrificed, as with the entrance behind the Fifth Third Bank building at 1 S. Dearborn St. in Chicago, where a notch was removed from the ground floor to essentially add an access lane to the existing narrow alley (off of W. Madison St.).

Some office towers are designed with access ramps parallel to the adjacent street. This design precludes storefront retail space, and should only be used in an alley.

Of course, smaller buildings simply do not have a driveway or alley to work with. In that case, pay close attention to how delivery and service vehicles make do. Vendors can be expected to raise prices for properties where the crew will be spending extra time to reach the dock or to cart materials to the building, or when the only practical access is after hours.

TRUCK TURNING TEMPLATE

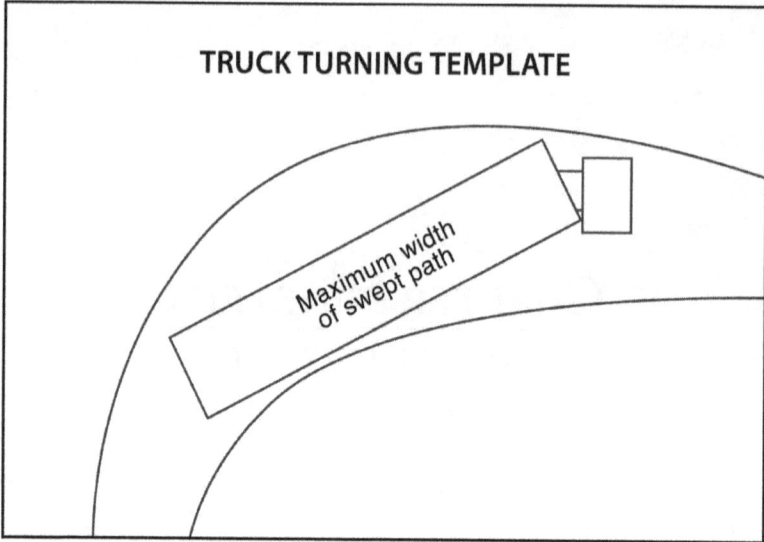

Maximum width of swept path

THREE CENTERED CURVE

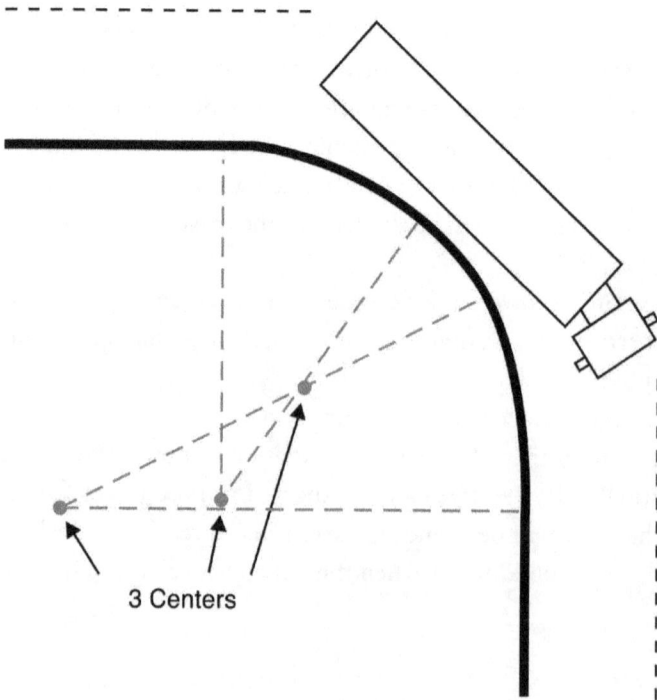

3 Centers

Chapter Twenty

INDUSTRIAL

For industrial uses, the access issues are broader than simply having room for trucks to make their wide turns into a site. Of equal importance, the trucks should have a clear route to a freeway, without having to cross through neighborhoods with incompatible streets and traffic. This problem increases as urban industrial areas become gentrified.

Chic lofts and industrial uses do not make good neighbors, and in growing cities the pressure against urban industrial uses is relentless. Elsewhere in this book I describe the need to be aware of potential changes to the streets and intersections serving a property, but for industrial uses, you must expand your research to include everything between the property and the freeway. It is not enough to know that the property zoning and the nearby streets are intended to remain industrial, because if the trucks must deal with urban congestion before reaching the open freeway, that directly affects the bottom line. This is one reason why in recent decades many industrial developments have sprouted far away from cities, but very close to freeway interchanges.

For the site access, you must know the maximum size truck that can safely make all necessary turns. Be sure to get opinions from an engineer and also from truckers serving the site.

THREE LEG DIRECTIONAL INTERCHANGE

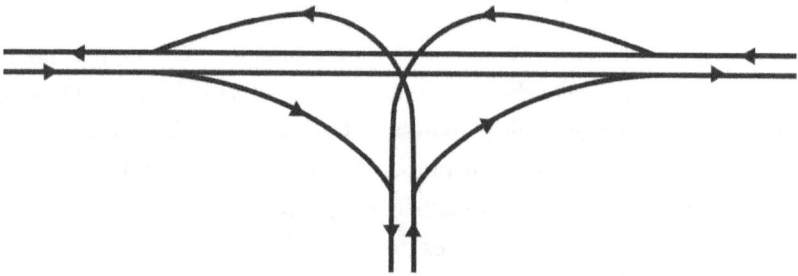

CHAPTER TWENTY-ONE

AIRPORTS

The larger urban airports are generally placed near a freeway (or a freeway is placed near them), and the first element of access is directing traffic from the freeway toward the airport, typically with an interchange that leads directly to the airport.

The airport entrance itself will alert drivers which lanes to use for access to the different airport uses, and each use should have its own entrance leading off of the main entrance. These entrances are arranged in order depending on the layout of the airport; however, the entrance to the passenger terminals is typically the last entrance.

The non-terminal uses include air freight, aircraft maintenance facilities, short and long term parking, employee parking, the control tower, administrative offices, private aviation, hotels, transit and taxi holding areas, and rental car lots. Each of these uses has its own particular needs. For now, the key point is that most of these uses should be easy to access from the main airport entrance street. Ideally, the main entrance street will not need to include any traffic signals or other perpendicular intersections, which slow the main flow of traffic leading to the terminal, and slip lanes are used whenever possible. These can be placed on the right or the left as conditions allow.

Most airports are, of course, laid out in loops. The main entrance street leads to the right edge of the passenger terminal, then arcs to the left across the front of the terminals and then continues arcing left until you are headed back out of the airport. Usually, a connection is included so vehicles can loop around the central portion of the airport continuously.

A critical access question is how many uses to place inside the main loop, which will determine the number of exit lanes that will be needed on the left side of the loop street. The uses placed inside the loop include short-term parking, transit, taxis, hotels, and preferably rental cars, all of which are vehicle intensive. Development inside the loop tends to be ever more dense and vertical, putting a premium on vehicle spaces, including access.

The uses located outside the loop often do not require direct access to the terminal, and include air freight, aircraft maintenance facilities, long-term parking, employee parking, and private aviation. This development tends to be single story.

For access from the main loop, the key issue is the location, visibility and spacing of the exits to the right (leading to uses outside the loop) and the left (leading to uses inside the loop). Note that larger vehicles will tend to be headed to areas outside the loop, whereas, cars comprise the vast majority of the vehicles headed inside the loop. The goal is for vehicles exiting the main entrance and loop to have an easy time of it, so that traffic keeps flowing freely.

To accomplish this goal, the vehicles must not only have a convenient exit, the exit must have capacity for a sufficient number of vehicles. We've all seen what happens to a freeway when vehicles attempting to exit cannot, usually because of an inadequate intersection at the end of the exit ramp. The same factors apply to internal streets at an airport, and they must be able to handle rush hour traffic without impeding traffic on the main entrance and loop.

Spacing of the exits will depend on several factors, but the most important is the speed of traffic. The slower the traffic, the more closely exists can be spaced. Some airports choose to have only one or two exits to the right, which lead to another street that is parallel with the entrance street. This configuration works well when the uses off to the right side are arranged in a lineal pattern parallel with the entrance street. When the uses off to the right are arranged perpendicular, they can still be served by a small number of exits, but the risk of congestion is increased, because these areas tend to only have one way to get to and from the main street.

Next we'll look at the various uses in turn, starting with air freight, because it is the most truck intensive, and working our way through the uses to long term parking, which has the fewest number of larger vehicles.

Air freight facilities are arranged much like smaller scale industrial parks. Freight is delivered into one side of the building by trucks and vans of all sizes. Pave about 85 or 90 feet from the face of the building for access to the loading dock. Freight goes out the back (the air side) of the building on airport vehicles, and sometimes planes will park close to the building as well. To maximize flexibility, pave about 500 or 600 feet out from the back of the buildings. Vehicles should have direct access from the back of the freight building to the internal street system on the tarmac, without having to travel on public streets.

After delivering the freight to the airport, the trucks must have an easy path back to the local street system and the freeway, but need not have access to the main loop street. It is preferable to keep delivery vehicles separate from the main loop street, which makes travel simpler and safer for both trucks and for the cars on the main loop street.

Aircraft maintenance facilities are often located at the far fringes of airports. They are always connected to the internal street system serving the tarmac, and sometimes they are connected directly to the local street system as well. That street system will be well away from the main loop street serving the terminals. Generous paved areas serve both planes and motor vehicles, and allow for the maximum flexibility for all users. Away from the planes, access and circulation should be designed like industrial parks, meaning that trucks should be able to come and go without difficulty. Parking is still required for employee vehicles and delivery vehicles of all sizes. Try to separate the parking for cars from the maneuvering area for trucks.

Private aviation facilities can also be located at the fringes of the airport. The key difference is that the planes are smaller, so the paved areas for maneuvering of planes and trucks can be smaller as well. The rule about keeping car parking areas separate remains; however, facilities serving VIPs will need to flexible, and provisions for getting cars onto the tarmac are preferred.

Long-term parking and employee parking can be located at the far end of the airport. These tend to be surface lots near the first exits off of the entrance streets. Once the cars are parked, shuttle buses carry people and luggage to the terminal, so the access question becomes whether shuttles use the main entrance and loop street or a different street. If there is enough space in the airport and enough shuttle traffic to justify it, a separate street is ideal. Surface parking is often a temporary placeholder until the airport develops more intensively; so wherever you see surface parking, think about how vertical development might eventually affect access.

It seems to me I spent my life in carpools, but you know, that's how I kept track of what was going on.

Barbara Bush

CHAPTER TWENTY-TWO

SUBURBAN SCHOOL

Schools function similar to corporate campuses, with rush hours during weekday mornings and afternoons. In addition, schools attract traffic in the evenings and weekends for extracurricular events, and the older the children, the more evening and weekend traffic. Because these events occur during off-peak hours, from an access perspective, the key thing is the morning and afternoon peak hours.

Depending on the surrounding street layout, there may be one or multiple access points. Generally speaking, when the school is on a corner, there is access from both streets.

If there is only one access point from a collector or arterial street, a signal is usually warranted if there are 1000 or more students. A key advantage of signals is that their timing can be programmed to facilitate the peak hour traffic. Nevertheless, a school district may be reluctant to pay for a signal, and feel compelled to operate without one, even where it is necessary based on objective engineering standards. The school district has more political influence than a typical private developer, and their pleas regarding a lack of money to pay for public street improvements (and related internal circulation features) may be persuasive. For the occasional district that is flush from a recent bond measure and building schools for the long term, the local transportation agency may allow installation of a signal for convenience, even if the traffic is less than is usually required for a warrant, with the expectation that the signal will be able to accommodate future school growth. In other words, the rules can be bent in either direction.

When schools are on local streets in residential neighborhoods, signals are not usually necessary, even when there are more than 1000 students, because the local street grid disperses the traffic. The tricky part in this setting is the buses. Most local streets cannot easily accommodate their turning movements, especially when on-street parking is allowed near the corners.

The internal circulation at newer schools mimics airports, in that lanes for dropping off and picking up passengers are just as important as parking. Ideally, the access separates incoming traffic into lanes for parking, passenger drop-offs, and buses. While airports have lengthy entrance streets for channeling traffic as needed, schools do not, so channelization is more challenging.

Separating incoming traffic consumes substantial amounts of real estate and money, which may be tight, and the throat becomes crucial. Sometimes, the throat simply isn't long enough or wide enough for smooth separation. In that case, buses are given priority during the peak periods, and sometimes are allowed to wait in fire lanes where parking is otherwise prohibited. Passenger vehicles must make do the best they can, though the local government will press the school to keep the vehicles waiting to pick up children in the afternoon from impeding street traffic, which naturally requires more space for parking on the school property. Several access points on different streets help to alleviate this congestion.

Older schools were built with smaller parking lots and less internal circulation space because a much lower percentage of children arrived by car, and at high schools, fewer students drove themselves to school. Now, these schools often experience parking challenges and traffic congestion, and in built up areas, there isn't much that can be done about it.

The internal circulation for schools will accommodate buses and fire trucks, so service and delivery vehicles should be able to get around without difficulty. Pay attention to theatre loading doors, and look for separation of loading areas. For example, is the stage loading door next to the waste storage, so service truck traffic is concentrated, or not?

Don't fight forces, use them.

Buckminster Fuller

AFTERWORD

All types of real estate rely on vehicle access to the surrounding street system, which compels real estate professionals to understand how access works. The most perplexing circumstances are where access is changing and extensive site renovations are required. When the changes are driven by site development and redevelopment, the developer must adjust their plans to complement the available access, however limited. Where access is being changed and the buildings are already in place, the challenge is that much greater.

The goal of this book is to inform the reader about the policies, practices and people that comprise this little corner of the real estate world. With this understanding of the back story, the professionals can proactively manage vehicle access to the mutual benefit of the properties involved and the traveling public. While ideal solutions are not always attainable, hopefully you will at least be able to recognize current and potential access problems, and respond accordingly.

Design is people.

Jane Jacobs

GLOSSARY

Acceleration Lane – An auxiliary lane, usually tapered, for the acceleration of vehicles preparing to merge into the through traffic lanes.

Access – The rights and ability for a vehicle to enter or exit a street. Formally known as rights of ingress and egress, informally known as a driveway or a curb cut.

Access Control – The extent to which the transportation agency (or toll road operator) restricts where vehicles may enter or exit a street. (In addition, access control means gates and other security measures that prevent the free flow of vehicles, but that type of access control is not covered in this book.)

Access Management – Limitation of the number, location, and type of access points to a street in an effort to improve traffic flow and safety.

Access Management Plan (AMP) – A formal street corridor plan to reduce the number of access points along a specified street segment.

Added Traffic – The additional traffic anticipated from developments or public works projects that are approved, but not yet completed or occupied.

Alignment – The horizontal and vertical plan of a street, as shown in plan and profile drawings. Plan drawings are as viewed from above, profile drawings are as viewed from the side.

ALTA (American Land Title Association) Survey – The most complete type of survey for commercial real estate, which shows access rights and restrictions in detail, among much other information.

Apron – The flared end of a driveway where it meets the street.

Area of Influence – The area around a project site that will be directly influenced by traffic going to the site or leaving the site, which usually becomes the area considered in a traffic study.

Arterial Street – A major thoroughfare serving higher speed through trips, with limited access to adjacent property.

Average Daily Traffic (ADT) – The average number of vehicles which use a street over a 24-hour period. This term also applies to the number of vehicle trips generated by a site or area over a 24-hour period.

Average Daily Trips (ADT) – The average number of vehicle trips generated during a 24-hour period from a specific site or area. This term also applies to traffic volumes on a street over a 24-hour period.

Below grade – A street or driveway located below the surface grade of the surrounding land. This circumstance requires ramps to make up the difference if you need to connect the two areas.

Bike Lane – A portion of a street reserved for use by bicycles; usually distinguished by striping, signing, and pavement markings.

Bus Bay – A widened area of street where buses pull over to pick up and drop off passengers.

Capacity – The maximum number of vehicles which can drive through a specified segment of a street during a specified time period; usually given in vehicles per hour or vehicles per day. At intersections, this is analyzed for each lane, including turning lanes.

Channelize – The use of traffic control devices, such as medians, pavement striping, turtle shell domes, and pork chops to separate or direct particular lanes of traffic.

Channelizing Island – A pork chop. (See the definition of pork chop below.)

Collector Street – A street which links many local streets to community centers or to the arterial system. They are one step below arterials and one step above local streets.

Commute Trips – Vehicle trips to work, including trips with intermediate stops when the final destination is either the home or the workplace.

Conflict Point – The point where two vehicles will collide unless one vehicle yields. Every access creates conflict points; the more lanes and turning movements allowed, the more conflict points.

Control Delay – The amount of delay in traffic caused when a traffic signal requires vehicles to slow or stop.

Corridor – A longitudinal geographic area usually defined around a street which includes the adjacent area served by the street. Commercial strips are often referred to as corridors.

Cross Slope – The slope of a street, driveway, or sidewalk that is perpendicular to the direction of travel.

Curb Cut – Short hand for driveway; literally any place where the curb line is interrupted.

Curb Extension – A sidewalk curb that extends out into an intersection forming a 270 degree arc; also known as a corner bulb.

Curb Return – The section of a curb which, at an intersection or driveway, angles or curves away from the curb along the main street.

Deceleration Lane – An auxiliary lane, usually tapered, for the slowing (deceleration) of vehicles preparing to turn off of a street.

Dedicate – To convey private property to public ownership for a public use; for example, to create a new street or widen an existing one.

Design Capacity – The maximum number of vehicles the traffic engineers expect to pass through a specified section of a street, usually given in vehicles per hour or vehicles per day. At intersections, this is specified for each lane, including turning lanes. This is distinguished from actual capacity, which is only confirmed after the street is built and operating.

Design Hourly Volume – The maximum number of vehicles the traffic engineers expect to be able to drive through a specified section of a street during an hour, usually the 30th highest hourly volume expected during the year.

Design Speed – The vehicle speed intended for a specific street design.

Design Standards – Specifications for such street design features as curvature, grades, pavement width, drainage facilities, etc.

Design Vehicle – The largest vehicle that an access or loading space is designed to accommodate, usually a truck of specified length.

Design Volume – Same as design capacity.

Detector Loop – A wire loop embedded in the pavement in the approach area of a signalized intersection, which senses passing vehicles, and sends that information to the signal controller.

Directional Split – The distribution of traffic on a two-way facility, usually expressed as a percentage of the total two-way traffic.

Divided Highway – A highway with separated lanes for traffic in opposite directions, such as when a median barrier has been installed.

Easement – A right of use over the property of another.

Egress – The provision of access out of a property or street. Providing access into the property is ingress.

Emergency Vehicle – Any vehicle used to respond to an incident or accident, such as police cars, fire engines, ambulances, and tow trucks.

Eminent Domain – The power of public agencies to take private property for a public use. Compensation must be provided to the property owner.

Encroachment – The intrusion of a structure which extends over a property line, easement boundary, or building setback line.

Expressway – A divided arterial highway for through traffic with full or partial control of access and generally with grade separations at major intersections.

Freeway – A divided highway with full access control and grade separation intended to serve through traffic and long distance trips.

Frontage Street – A street parallel and adjacent to a freeway or expressway that provides access to the local street system and property.

Functional Classification – The system for classification of street types.

Geometry or Geometric Design – The detailed design of a street or driveway, which provides mathematical information in plan and profile view of the street and driveway surfaces regarding angles, radii, vertical and horizontal curves, dimensions, etc.

Grade – The elevation of the land or street surface. For driveways, the grade is specified as the percentage rise in elevation; for example, 3% grade is a 3 foot rise in elevation over a distance of 100 feet.

Grade Separation – An overpass or underpass.

Green Book (The) – The standard reference of street design, published by the American Association of State Highway and Transportation Officials (AASHTO).

Highway Capacity Manual – The standard reference for street and freeway capacity, published by the Transportation Research Board, a federal government entity.

Horizontal Alignment – The design of a street as seen from above (the plan view).

Horizontal Curve – A curve in the street to the right or left on the horizontal plane (as distinguished from vertical curve).

Horizontal Development – Property improvements that do not extend above ground level, including subsurface utilities, streets, sidewalks, etc.

Induced Demand – The additional traffic created over the long-term when a street improvement, such as a new freeway, gradually draws new development to an area.

Ingress – The provision of access into a property. Providing access out to the street is egress.

Interchange – The intersection of a freeway with a street, highway, or another freeway.

Intersection Functional Area – The segments of street on all legs of an intersection that are influenced by the operation of the intersection.

Interstate – A divided freeway for through traffic with full control of access limited to interchanges that is part of the federally designated system of interstate and defense highways.

Lane – The area of a street, usually indicated by pavement stripes, intended for one line of vehicles.

Lane Group – The lanes approaching an intersection from one direction.

Latecomer Ordinance – An ordinance that allows for an early developer to build extra street (or other public utility) capacity, and be reimbursed later by neighbors who develop later.

Latent Demand – The additional traffic from existing development that will use a new or improved street once it is built.

Level of Service (LOS) – A measure of traffic congestion, as defined by the Highway Capacity Manual. The levels range from A to F, with A representing no congestion and F representing very congested traffic.

Limited Access Highway – A highway without a right of access except where specified (usually only at signalized intersections).

Linked Trip – A vehicle trip that is one link among many, as when a vehicle drives around on several errands.

Local Street – A street primarily for access to abutting property.

Median – The area or obstacle (such as raised curbs or a planter strip) of a divided freeway or street that separates the traffic flowing in opposite directions.

Mobility Standards – The standards for maximum allowable traffic congestion, usually expressed as a numerical Volume to Capacity Ratio (VC Ratio), or as a graded Level of Service (LOS) ranging from A for no congestion to F for very congested traffic.

Mode Split – The percentages of person trips (or vehicle trips) using different modes of transportation, such as pedestrian, bicycle, bus, plane, rail, and automobiles. The total adds up to 100 percent.

Mountable Curb – A curb with a sloped face which allows vehicles to ride over the curb, often seen in the center of roundabouts, and on corners where the rear wheels of trucks may not always fit in the travel lane.

Near-Side Stop – A transit stop located on the approach to (before) an intersection.

Non-Commute Trips – Trips made for purposes other than work, such as shopping, school, and recreation.

Off-Peak Direction of Travel – The direction of travel with less traffic during a peak commuting period.

Off-Peak Period – The time outside the peak commuting periods, including the midday, evening, night, and early morning. Saturday may or not be outside the peak period, depending on the location.

Off-Tracking – The path followed by the rear wheels of turning vehicles, especially trucks or trailers (cars have minimal off-tracking). The longer the truck or trailer, the wider the off-tracking, and thus the wider the street surface should be where these vehicles turn.

PAAL – Parking Area Access Lane.

Parking Lane – An auxiliary lane for the on-street parking of vehicles.

Partial Taking – The taking of a portion of a property under eminent domain.

Peak Direction and Peak Direction of Travel – The direction with a majority of traffic during a peak period.

Peak Hour – The one-hour time period in the morning, and the one hour time period in the afternoon, when the maximum traffic occurs. On Saturday, this occurs during the middle of the day.

Peak Period – The time period, surrounding and including the peak hour in the morning and in the afternoon, when the heaviest demand occurs on a specified street. It usually lasts two to four hours.

Peripheral Parking – A parking lot or garage located adjacent to a downtown or other major activity center.

Plat – A recorded land division survey (subdivision or partition) which shows the boundaries of individual parcels of land together with streets and easements. Plats are approved by government officials and are not to be confused with county tax authority maps which are often called by the same name. Access rights and restrictions may be specified on a plat.

Platoon – A cluster of vehicles traveling together which is formed by one green-cycle of a traffic signal.

Pork Chop – A raised island separator, usually roughly triangular in shape, used to funnel turning movements, especially for access that is limited to right-in, right-out. More formally known as a type of "channelizing island."

Preliminary Engineering or Preliminary Design – Early drafts of a street design.

Queue – A line of waiting vehicles, such as those stopped at a red light.

Queue Length – The length of a queue, used to measure the need for storage lanes and intersection spacing.

Radial Highway – An arterial highway leading to or from an urban center.

Restricted Access – A driveway that accommodates only some turning movements. Left turns out of a driveway are the most likely to be prohibited, followed by left turns in.

Reverse Commute – The commute trips in the opposite direction of the majority of traffic during a peak period. Travel from a central city area to a suburb in the morning is one example of a reverse commute trip.

Street – The portion of a right-of-way, including shoulders, for vehicular use.

Sag Grade – The low point where two slopes meet, often seen where a driveway meets a street. When the slopes are too steep, the bumper of vehicles and/or trailer tongues will scrape on the pavement.

Sight Distance – The line of sight available to the driver approaching a cross street. The required minimum sight distance increases along with the speed limit.

Sight Distance Triangle – Same as Vision Clearance Triangle

Signal Priority – The programmable priority given to various movements through a signalized intersection, such as when, and for how long, a left turn arrow will be green.

Signal Progression – A series of traffic signals synchronized to allow the continuous flow of vehicles.

Single Occupant Vehicle (SOV) – A car occupied by one person.

Signal Warrant – The amount of traffic (among other factors) required to justify installation of a traffic signal.

Site Plan – A scaled drawing showing uses and structures for a parcel of land. A site plan should include lot lines, buildings, access driveways, parking areas, landscape features, and utility lines.

Skew – The angle where a driveway meets the street, measured in degrees away from perpendicular. A driveway that is 80° from the street has a 10° skew. (Also used for public street intersections.)

Slip Lane – A deceleration lane for right turns where there is some type of median at the driveway entrance to separate the lane from other traffic.

Spacing Standards – Regulations for the minimum distance between two accesses, between an access and a street intersection, and between street intersections.

Spillback – Traffic that requires more than one green light cycle to move through an intersection.

Storage Lane – An auxiliary lane for vehicles waiting to turn at a signalized intersection.

Taking – A common synonym for condemnation or any substantial interference with private property rights by government.

Three-Centered Curve – A modified type of radius curb return that accommodates the off-tracking of truck turns. Comprised of three arcs, it is not perfectly round like a radius curb.

Throat – The area of an entrance between the street access and the first intersecting driveway or parking space. The throat serves as storage lanes for vehicles entering and exiting a property.

Throughput – The volume of vehicles or passengers passing a specific point during a specified time period.

Traffic Assignment – The estimated distribution of trip routes on a street network, which is used for analysis of the traffic pattern. Traffic engineers estimate the percentage of vehicles using various routes to a property.

Traffic Count – A count of vehicles passing a given point during a specified time period.

Traffic Engineering – The determination of the required capacity and conceptual layout of streets.

Traffic Impact Analysis (TIA) – An engineering study that evaluates and forecasts the traffic effects of a proposed development or public works project.

Traffic Study – Same as Traffic Impact Analysis.

Traffic Volume – The number of vehicles on a transportation facility.

Transportation Demand Management (TDM) – The strategies and techniques for reducing the number of vehicles on the street, especially during rush hour. Techniques include incentives, such as subsidized transit, and disincentives, such as higher gasoline taxes and parking rates.

Trip – A one-direction movement of a vehicle from the origin to the destination.

Trip Generation Rates – The number of vehicle trips to and from a development, per units of measure such as thousand square feet, housing unit, or employee. The rates published by the Institute of Transportation Engineers (ITE) are the standard reference used to estimate the traffic impacts of proposed development.

Unlinked Trip – A vehicle trip directly from the origin to the destination that does not include any intermediate stops.

Unrestricted Access – A driveway that accommodates all turning movements for both ingress and egress, including left turns.

Vehicle Occupancy – The number of people in a vehicle.

Vertical Alignment – The street design as viewed from the side (the profile view, often shown in a distorted scale).

Vertical Crest – The highest point of a vertical curve. If the curve is too sharp, the underside of vehicles will scrape on the crest.

Vertical Curve – A vertical rise or drop in the street grade, as with a hill or dip. Vertical rises restrict sight distance. If the vertical curve of a drop is too sharp, that is a sag grade.

Vision Clearance Triangle – The triangular area at driveway corners and intersection that must be kept free of visual obstructions so drivers exiting can see cross traffic, and vice versa. The size of the triangle increases with the speed limit on the cross street.

Volume to Capacity Ratio (VC Ratio) – The ratio of the actual number of vehicles to the capacity of a transportation facility, especially an intersection.

Weaving – When multiple vehicles traveling the same direction change lanes in the same segment of street; that is, some merge to the left while others merge to the right. This occurs where access points are too close together.